ISBN 978-1-330-18547-6
PIBN 10047304

1 MONTH OF
FREE
READING

at

www.ForgottenBooks.com

By purchasing this book you are eligible for one month membership to ForgottenBooks.com, giving you unlimited access to our entire collection of over 700,000 titles via our web site and mobile apps.

To claim your free month visit: www.forgottenbooks.com/free47304

A FIRST BOOK

IN

WRITING ENGLISH

BY

EDWIN HERBERT LEWIS, Ph.D.

ASSOCIATE PROFESSOR OF ENGLISH IN LEWIS INSTITUTE
AND IN THE UNIVERSITY OF CHICAGO

15698

New York

THE MACMILLAN COMPANY

LONDON: MACMILLAN & CO., Ltd.

1897

Norwood Press
J.   Cushing & Co. — Berwick & Smith
Norwood Mass. U S.A.

PREFACE

It sometimes happens that the study of the principles of composition is left until the overcrowded last year of the high school, under the plea that facts ought to precede generalizations. Is it not better to have the pupil begin two or three years earlier than this to frame simple generalizations for his own future guidance? The first year student daily awakes to new experiences and problems. He demands rules and reasons: "*How* shall he choose theme topics? *How much* shall he put into a sentence? *Why* is *electrocution* in bad usage?" If the principle is asked for, should it not be given — as much of it as can be digested? When such a course is followed, time enough is left in the high school for composition to become a habit. The complex process wherein invention, as it proceeds, is rectified by criticism, involves many delicate reflexes. The formulated principle, invaluable to the student in revising, in turn grows to be an unconscious factor in every succeeding act of composition.

The more essential rules ought not to be mere phantoms to the boy just completing his first year

in the secondary school. In regard to other matters of living, great principles are taught him from
infancy, without the slightest fear of setting up too
analytic a state of mind. If a boy of three may be
told "always to do one thing at a time," must a
boy be eighteen before he is told "always to
write about one thing at a time"? At three the
child is required to control some of his strongest
emotions; must he be eighteen before he is asked
to check digressions in the paragraph? And is it
possible to implant a genuine habit of checking
digressions except by leading the student from
particular instances to some generalization which
he may keep in mind as a norm for future self-
criticism? Synthesis and analysis cannot safely
be separated; a good prescription for most rhetorical disorders is, more of both. Indeed, what seems
to be needed to-day in teaching composition is not
one thing, but several: on the one hand, more
utilization of literature and more appeal to social
interests; on the other hand, more inductions and
generalizations by the student himself; on both
hands, more time for practice and self-criticism.

In the present book, originally printed privately
for my own classes and now rewritten and enlarged,
I have tried to present a large number of definite
situations to be faced for constructive practice both
in organization and in diction; and to give in
simple, even colloquial language, all the larger

generalizations which a boy presenting himself at college might reasonably be expected to have been using for two or three years as touchstones of his own work. Except in the chapters on punctuation and grammar, the order of reaching generalizations is meant to be essentially inductive. In these review-chapters a part of the principles come before the illustrations in order to get the help of all past associations. Even here the induction is often gone through with a second time, leading up to a restatement of the principle. It is recommended that students should often be asked to frame generalizations of their own, though the textbook may have led up to similar ones. In Chapters VII. and X., on words, I have tried to present conditions favorable to the framing of definitions by the student. By various devices I have constantly tried to avoid separation between exercise critical and exercise constructive. Occasionally, after the correct form has been studied, bad English is offered for correction, for the sake of the appeal to the student's personal pride and his sense of the ridiculous; but in general it is assumed that the student's correction of his own bad English will afford plenty of contact with faulty forms.

The book is primarily intended to be used in close connection with the literary studies of the first two years of the secondary course. It may be used later if the arrangement of subjects allows little time for literature in these earlier years. The order of presentation should,[1] in the author's opinion, follow that of the book. Still, Chapter VIII., on correct choice of words, may be taken at the start if the teacher prefers. Where a good deal of literary study is carried on in the first year, the first eight chapters are perhaps enough for this year. But a rate of progress cannot be prescribed. A text-book is a mere help, and bad in proportion as it tries to be anything more. Its function seems to be to supply the supplementary appeal to the eye, since the living teacher can engage to do this but to a limited extent. It appears obvious that the book should be read slowly enough to permit two things — much parallel literary study, and much revision of themes in the light of preceding chapters. First drafts are sometimes all that are worth making; but usually a task requiring connected discourse is not finished until there have been several revisions. If the student writes each new composition with a view to one particular kind of excellence, and then revises with reference to the kinds of excellence he has previously striven for, he will gradually be able to hold several stylistic principles in mind as he composes. Many themes should be written in class. A limited pe-

---

[1] From the first, brief supplementary themes, especially reproductions, should be required. For bibliography of material, see Chapter XIII.

riod should be set for the first draft; and half as much time may well be spent in revising before this is handed in. In this revision the student may profitably read his theme as many times as there are chapters to be mentally reviewed.

The remarkable strength of the verbal memory in students of the first two years of the secondary school is a fact by which every teacher must have been impressed.[1] Add to this fact the other, that the pupil's social interests are now in a perfect renaissance of liveliness, and you have exactly the conditions for enlarging the working vocabulary. It is now or never. The boy, though like the man he hates a fine distinction in conversation, is growing out of the exaggerated reticence which has of late seemed to him the manly thing. He is no longer determined to employ what Mrs. Meynell, speaking of the boy of twelve, calls his "carefully shortened vocabulary."[2] The girl, even more than the boy, is full of new ideas which would flower into speech if the words were to be had. To capture these new interests and satisfy them by literature is of course the best thing. Study of isolated words, whether for knowledge or for power, is but supplementary to the study of the vital functions of words in the living organism. But even the study of synonyms, if pursued in preparation for

[1] Cf. President Stanley Hall's *Pedagogical Seminary*, iv. i. 76.
[2] *The Children*, p. 103. (*The Bodley Head.* John Lane.)

an oral debate, — one of the very best exercises for first-year students, — or in connection with a page of spirited prose, rapidly becomes constructive and vital. Although the chapters on vocabulary (IX. and X.) may be given before the student has begun a foreign language, the best results with them will not be secured until he has had at least six months in Latin. The study of prefixes and suffixes (p. 186 ff.) should not be made burdensome. Some general view of the subject seems desirable, but the detailed study is best given in connection with an interesting context.

For kindly criticism or advice I have debts of gratitude to Professor and Mrs. W. D. McClintock; to Professor F. A. March, Professor John Dewey, and Professor Robert Herrick; to several of my colleagues, especially Director George M. Carman, Miss Jane Noble, and Mr. Phil B. Kohlsaat; to Mr. F. A. Manny, to Mrs. Hufford and Miss Dye, of Indianapolis; to Superintendent A. F. Nightingale, Miss Jones, and Miss Herrick, of the Chicago high schools. I have been particularly indebted to Carpenter's *Advanced Exercises,* a book made familiar to me by using it with freshmen in college; and to Scott & Denney's *Paragraph-Writing.* For the index I have to thank Miss L. E. W. Benedict, librarian of Lewis Institute, and Mr. Lewis Gustafson.

E. H. L.

Chicago, April 15, 1897.

CONTENTS

INTRODUCTORY EXPLANATIONS

15698

Our plan provides for a good many short compositions. These, as well as all other exercises should be written on uniform theme-paper,[1] say eight inches by ten, with a broad margin at both sides. There are advantages in the double margin. First, it is easier for the reader of the theme to jot down his suggestions at the right, since he need not turn the paper to do so. Secondly, it is well for the student to learn the knack of keeping *a straight edge* at the left hand. Only one side of the paper should be written on. If a mistake is made, a heavy line may be drawn through the word. The manuscript ought to present the neatest possible appearance. Blank spaces are to be avoided at the end of lines, except where a paragraph ends. The straight edge, referred to above, is to be scrupulously preserved at the left of the page, except that when a new paragraph (that is, division of the theme) is to begin, the first line of it should start about two inches farther to the right than the other lines. The pages should be carefully numbered in the upper right-hand cor-

[1] Some teachers will prefer to use composition-books.

B   1

ner, and kept in their proper order. Nothing is more disconcerting to any person who reads a manuscript than to open the paper and find before him the last page, rather than the first. Every theme should have a definite title. This should appear in the blank space at the top of the first page and in the endorsement of the folded paper, on the back of the last page. The theme should be folded once, lengthwise. In the blank space at the top should be written the endorsement, which should follow this model: (1) name; (2) name of course; (3) title; (4) date.

> Richard Doe.
> First year English.
> A Dialogue on Politics.
> Oct. 1, 189–.

After the themes have been read, whether by the instructor alone or by the class and the instructor, they will be returned with marginal comments, and (just under the endorsement) a summary of these comments. In many cases the student will be expected to rewrite, and the word *Rewrite* will appear with the general comment. Otherwise he will be expected to *Revise,* that is, to interline corrections and improvements on the manuscript without copying it.

Each student's papers will be filed and kept. He will often be asked to consult with the instructor concerning his own progress, as shown by his bundle of themes.

The following suggestive signs [1] may be used in the margin of themes, indicating the presence of errors, the actual errors to be discovered by the pupil for himself. Some teachers will prefer a simpler system of symbols, some a more elaborate system. The suggested list can easily be modified or supplanted.

Ms. Bad manuscript.

✓. Some obvious fault — a mark which will be used more and more frequently as the student's knowledge increases. The check-mark will frequently indicate bad spelling or punctuation, or fault in capitalizing.

Sp. Bad spelling (see under check-mark). .

Hy. Fault in use of hyphen.

P. Fault in punctuation (see also under check-mark).

Cap. Fault in the use of a capital letter (see check-mark).

L. Too loose ; structure rambling.

S. Solecism.

C. Structure incoherent.

E. *Lack of emphasis in sentence.*

U. *Lack of unity in sentence.*

Tr. Transpose order of words.

V. Vague.

A. Ambiguous.

¶U. *Lack of unity in paragraph.*

¶. Proper place for a paragraph.

(. Run two paragraphs together.

[]. Passages within brackets to be omitted.

𝒹. Dele, take out, omit ; a mark used in correcting printer's proof.

[1] A part of these signs are from G. R. Carpenter's admirable *Exercises in Rhetoric and English Composition.*

.	Against a passage requiring to be wholly recast.
Ri.	Unnecessary repetition of idea.
?.	Questions truth of statement.
B.	Barbarism.
I.	Impropriety.
W.	Wordy.
H.	High-flown, inflated, or over-ambitious.
D.	Consult the dictionary.
Hack.	Hackneyed.
Bw.	Better word needed — a more exact or appropriate word.
Rw.	Unnecessary repetition of a word.
M.	Metaphors mixed, or other fault in the use of figures of speech.
K.	Awkward, ugly, or unpleasing.
Bt.	Bad taste.

A strong notebook of portable size is needed for the work in spelling and vocabulary. It should be used from the first for noting new words, etc. See page 199.

A FIRST BOOK

WRITING ENGLISH

CHAPTER I

THE ART OF WRITING ENGLISH

An Art of Communication. — Language may be studied in various ways. It may be scientifically investigated as a historical growth, or as a curious revelation of how the human mind works. This kind of study has pure knowledge for its object; if it learns the laws which govern language, it is satisfied. Again, language may be studied with a view to applying its principles to the art of self-expression. The attempt to find words for one's ideas has enlivened many a weary hour for many a person who wrote merely for his own satisfaction. But the chief object for which language should be studied is that it may be made a means of communication.

Most that is good in life comes from men's ability

to make their fellows share their thoughts and feelings. But it is not always an easy thing to make others see how we feel or think. The young child is called an *infant,* a word which means *not-speaking.* Half his miseries arise from his inability to communicate his notions. "Men are but children of a larger growth," and much of their misery results from inability to tell what they think or feel. In a sense the case is worse for the man than for the child. The latter makes gestures and grimaces to help his meaning out; and he depends not in vain on pitch and stress. The grown man is partly shorn of these helps, in that he has to communicate by letters and other compositions. How much more work the eye does to-day than the ear! Before the age of printing, things were different.

Both in speaking and in writing there are many special laws that must be observed if there is to be real communication. The special laws of spoken language are not so numerous as those of written language. Written language has to be much more careful than spoken; the writer has no chance of correcting himself on the spot if not understood. Nevertheless a knowledge of how to communicate by written words is a very great help in communicating orally.

The art of communicating by means of written English words is called English composition, or rhetoric. The latter word once meant the art of speaking; and it still keeps this sense when a composition is written to be delivered. Rhetoric is a useful art, like that of curing the sick, or that of building bridges. A matter of prime importance to each man is that, in business or in society, he should be able to say or write exactly what he means; rhetoric helps him to do this. A business man may lose money by failing to make himself clearly understood; misunderstandings and quarrels arise between friends because some one has failed to write just what he meant; a man is liable to be taken for a boor if he abuses the English language. Rhetoric is an exceedingly practical art.

It would not, however, be fair to remove all emphasis from the fact that rhetoric is a fine art, an art of beauty. As soon as the student begins to master the use of words, he has a chance to become an artist in language. In producing a beautiful thing he feels the artist's pleasure. Most persons like to play some musical instrument, or experiment in color, or use a camera. Why should they not come to enjoy the art of setting down their ideas in words skilfully chosen, and arranged with delicate precision? The old Greeks enjoyed it — those people who knew how to extract so much high pleasure from life. Along with their musical contests and athletic contests, they had trials of skill in poetry and in public speech.

There is no more delightful art than that of

writing, if the writer finds words for his own fresh impressions. In order to learn the mandolin, a new player will train his wrist till it aches. But thrumming music is doubtless small pleasure compared with writing music; and writing English is in a way like writing music, — a fine, high, creative process, which, in the hands of a master, results in a permanent, not a fleeting, product.

A teacher of English recently said that, in a certain sense, if a student likes any study at all he can be brought to like composition also.[1] She was right. If he cares for mathematics, and the beautiful precision by which everything in mathematics falls exactly into its place, he will enjoy showing the exact relations he conceives to exist between the parts of his sentence. If a girl likes music she will care for the music that is in prose. She will perceive that a good sentence is free from ugly sounds, and has furthermore a music of rhythm, a finely modulated rise and fall that a keen ear readily perceives. A lad declares himself interested in inventing or in building machinery. If so, why should he not enjoy building a theme? To think out a new mechanical device requires much the same kind of ingenuity, sense of proportion, perception of cause and effect, that

---

[1] Elizabeth H. Spalding: *The Problem of Elementary Composition.* Boston, D. C. Heath & Co.

are required in thinking out the logical framework of a composition.

The student should work steadily toward the
point where he may come to have an abiding love
for that which is lucid and beautiful in expression
by words. He will never regret the time he
spends in perfecting his instrument of expression.
No matter how practical the life he plans to lead,
the power of writing down his ideas in good
English, in a way that will leave no doubt as
to what he meant and how earnestly he meant
it, will always profit him. One meets everywhere men who lament that they gave so little
attention to our language when they were young
enough to master it.

The Limitations of the Art. — It must never be
supposed that, because to some extent a fine art,
rhetoric should be studied as an end in itself. What
was said a moment ago about the primary aim
of the study must be kept steadily in view. We
study the art of composition not for the art's
sake, but to communicate our ideas and feelings.
Rhetoric does not profess to supply the student
with ideas, though it assumes that his mind is
stimulated to new thought by trying to express that
which he already has. The more ideas he brings
to the study, — ideas he has thought out in
life or in his other studies, like literature, history,

civics, — the more facility he will carry away; for ideas are the very best of material to make themes of. If composition does only one thing for a given person, — if, namely, it brings him to a sturdy habit of *finding something to say* before he asks other people to listen to him, — it is eminently worth while.

Write for an Audience. — Writing is usually good in proportion as the writer is interested in it. If he cares for it, if he is anxious to find a worthy thought and make it clear to the eyes of others, he will be very likely to succeed in doing so. Something of every student's weekly work ought to be good enough to come before the eyes of his friends and to command his friends' respect. The student will find that his mates are keen critics; they will not respect poor work. But they are also fair and sympathetic critics, ready and willing to surrender on sight to really good work. A class as a whole will judge the compositions of each member disinterestedly and appreciatively.

Whatever is most characteristic of you, as different from other people; whatever gift is yours, of imagination, or reasoning power, or emotion, or humor, — all will find its fit expression in your writing. Every human being is particularly interested in something, is peculiarly apt at something. To find out what most appeals to one's self in literature or in life, and to voice one's ideas about it, is to know a keen pleasure. It is more. It is to be of some use to one's fellows. As human beings we want other human beings to tell us the best that is in them. If a man has ideas we wish to share them — and wish him to learn how to express them that we may share them. If he hasn't ideas the effort to express what he considers such will convince both him and us of the fact. But then! — everybody has ideas.

CHAPTER II

ON READING ALOUD, AND ON SPELLING

Reading Aloud. — One of the quickest ways of learning to know good English, is oral reading. For him who would write the language it is therefore a great economy to learn to read it. It is an invaluable habit to read aloud every day some piece of prose with the finest feeling the reader can lend to it. In no other way can one so easily learn to notice and to remember new words. In no other way can one catch the infinitely varied rhythm of prose, and acquire a sense of how a good sentence rises gradually from the beginning and then descends in a cadence. This rise and fall of the sentence is not merely a matter of voice; it is a matter of thought as well. Similarly, the law of unity in the sentence, a law which prescribes what shall constitute a complete thought, is curiously bound up with the laws of the human voice. A clause that is too long to be pronounced in a single breath is usually clumsy in logic. In the next place, reading aloud helps one to spell correctly. Furthermore, it is the best means of detecting those useless repetitions which betray poverty of vocabulary.

Rousseau called accent the soul of language. If the student reads aloud from writers whose work was natural, unforced, original, he will gradually come to see his own ideas more clearly, feel his own feelings more keenly. Best of all, however, let him read his own work aloud, habitually. This will help him to see whether or not it is correct, natural, effective.

Spelling.[1] — Bad spelling should practically be a thing of the past for each student by the end of his first high school year. Every one can learn to spell, though some more rapidly than others

Perhaps the chief reason why persons fail to spell correctly is that they do not read correctly. They have not trained their eyes to see what is on the page; they do not notice the syllables. It is a good practice to read every day a page or two very slowly, examining the words letter by letter. It is equally helpful to read the page aloud after examining it. In so doing give every vowel its true value; cut no syllable short that should be sounded distinctly.

After writing a theme, go through it, challenging the spelling. Do not hand in your work without having consulted your own dictionary. A bad

---

[1] Do not discard your old text-book in grammar or in "language." Bring it to school and keep it at hand for ready reference. In it are rules for spelling; these, as well as other rules, you will be glad to review occasionally.

speller may not be able to win in an oral spelling-match; but there is no reason why every page of his writing should not be perfect in orthography.

Into a little blank-book copy the correct form of every word you misspell. Each day read over carefully several words by syllables, and then write them from memory. The more frequently the hand writes the word in its correct form, the better; for the hand has a memory of its own, and the mere act of writing a given form tends to fix it in memory.

Make good spelling a matter of pride. Habitual bad spelling is a slovenly thing, a mark of illiteracy.

Spelling of Compound Words. — It may be well to call attention here to the use of the hyphen in compound words.

1. The hyphen is needed in a compound adjective, if there is any doubt as to the meaning when the hyphen is omitted. "Red-hot iron" may be a different idea from "red hot iron."

2. Numbers like the following take the hyphen: seventy-three, seventy-third.

3. Many a word once compounded is now written solid, that is, as a single word: railroad, steamboat, anybody, anything, raindrop, forever, schoolboy, schoolhouse, schoolmate, schoolfellow (but school days, school teacher, school district); myself, yourself (but one's self); childlike, lifelike. All these

words but two, it will be seen, have a monosyllable for the first part. When in doubt as to whether or not a hyphen is needed, consult some special manual like Bigelow's *Handbook of Punctuation.*

In all your writing, join distinctly syllables that you wish to have go .together· Notice the absurd and misleading effect of such careless writing as this: "He was a glass maker and worked down at the glass house; his gal lant moust ache and his loud voice trai ned by blow ing glass mad e him wel come at the harvest home celebrations."

Possessives. — The possessive singular of a monosyllable ending in *s* is regularly made by adding '*s*, pronounced as an extra syllable. Thus: Jones's; Briggs's. For the polysyllable ending in *s* or the sound of *s*, merely the apostrophe is usually required, as in the plural. Thus: "Moses' seat"; "conscience' sake."

Singulars and Plurals. — Spell aloud by syllables, and write from dictation the plurals of the following? ˙Analysis, animalcule, antithesis, appendix, bandit, cherub, crisis, ellipsis, focus, fungus, genus, hypothesis, madame, memorandum, monsieur, mother-in-law, mussulman, nebula, oasis, parenthesis, radius, spoonful, synopsis.

What are the singulars — if singulars there are — of data, errata, magi, strata, vertebræ?

Written Exercise. — Below are given the correct form of certain words often misspelled by pupils in the first and second years of a secondary school. Without previous study write each word from dictation. Afterwards spell aloud by syllables each word that you misspelled in writing from dictation. Then write at least twenty times the correct form. The object is to acquire a kind of automatic correctness. In composing, one should have his mind free for thought; one should not have to think much more about spelling than about breathing.

Accompany; advisability; all right; anniversary; appearance; associated; bargained; buried; carriage; catarrh; cemetery; characteristic; commander; commotion; conceive; condescension; confidants; confidence; deceive; describe; descriptions; despair; difficulty; dilapidate; disappointed; disappeared; ecstasy; enemies; enemy; exaggerate; excrescence; existence; fascination; fatiguing; finally; further; grammar; handkerchief; hating; hemorrhage; immature; indispensable; irresistible; lightning; literary; living; loathsome; lose (the money); manœuvre; melancholy; minister; ministry; misshapen; necessary; niece; occurrence; offered; opportunity; outrageous; parallel; paralysis; peaceable; persuade; planned; poniard; primitive; principal (objection); principle (of action); privilege; promenading; pursuit; received; recommend; redoubtable; referred;

representatives; rhythm; sacrilegious; secretary; seize; seized; separate; shoeing; siege; simile; stopped; striking; studied; superintendent; supposing; tenants; theatre; their (money); transferred; until; veil (on face); vengeance; very; village; wasn't; whether; Roger de Coverley; George Eliot; Lord Macaulay; Michigan; Thackeray.

Word-Breaking. — At the end of a line do not divide (*a*) a monosyllable, (*b*) a short dissyllable, such as *real, doing.* Divide polysyllables according to their etymological composition (to be found in the dictionary). Some authors discountenance beginning a second line with -*ic*, -*al*, -*ing*, -*ly*. These breakings are perhaps permissible, *if the hyphen is made very distinct.*

Written and Oral Exercise. — The instructor should ask each pupil in turn to recall, spell, and pronounce some word that doubles the letter *c*. The class should then be given a few minutes to write from memory as many of those given as they can recall. After this the pronouncing and spelling should proceed as long as possible, alternately with the writing. The lists should then be compared, and the pupil who has reproduced the largest number of words should be asked to spell and pronounce each one on his list. The other pupils should then be called upon to read from

their own lists words that the first fails to give.
Each should then be asked to add to his paper all
words remembered by other members of the class
but not by him.[1]

Pronunciation. — A person who regards good usage
in pronunçiation and who articulates with unaffected
nicety, is received at once as an educated man. It
is interesting to see how often Lord Chesterfield,
the best-mannered of Englishmen, insists that a
gentleman is known by his accent. Chesterfield's
letters to his son are full of this idea. A sense
of ease and security blesses him who knows how
to sound every word that occurs to him as he talks;
it is such a sense as a man feels when he is sure
that his clothes fit him and are cut according to
the accepted conventions. It is accordingly worth
all the trouble involved, to form a habit of letting
no word pass unchallenged as to its orthoëpy.
Look it up in the dictionary, or in a good manual like
Phyfe's *Seven Thousand Words often Mispronounced.*

Exercise. — Below is given a short list of words
frequently mispronounced. The instructor should
pronounce the words, and ask the class to pronounce them.

---

[1] The author is indebted for the idea of this exercise to Miss
Catherine Aiken's *Methods of Mind-Training* (Harper & Bros.).
If it proves helpful it should be extended to the consonants *d,
f, g, l, m, n, p, r, s, t.*

Abdomen,

abject,

absinthe,

abstruse,

acacia,

accessory,

acclimate

acoustics,

actor,

adagio,

adult,

advertisement,

aëronaut,

again,

aged,

aggrandize,

aide-de-camp,

allopathy,

ally,

alma mater

alternate (noun and adjective),

amenable,

apricot,

arbutus,

aroma,

aspirant,

bade,

bellows,

biography,

bitumen,

boatswain,

bravado,

bronchitis

canine,

cant,

can't,

cement (noun),

cemetery,

cerebrum,

clematis,

coadjutor

daunt,

decade

devil,

diphtheria

disdain,

dislike,

drama,

duke,

dynasty,

enervate,

evil

exhale,

exhaust,

extant,

extempore,

finale,

finance,

financier,

garrulous

gaunt,

genuine,

gibber,

gibbet,

glacier,

gratis,

grimace,

half,

hegira,

heinous

impious,

jugular,

lamentable

learned (adj.)

legend,

lever,

literature,

nape,

nomad,

opponent,

pageant,

patriot,

patron,

petal,

precedence,

precedent,

quay,
revolt
rise (noun),
sacrifice,

squalor,
subtile,
subtle,
vagary,

water,
wrath,
zoölogy.[1]

Abélard,
Abernethy,
About (Edmond),
Abydos,
Acheron,
Achitophel,
Adonis,
Ægean,
Æolus,
Æschylus,
Afghanistan,
Agincourt,
Agnes,
Aguilar (Grace)
Aïda,
Aix-la-Chapelle,
Alaric,

Alcantara,
Alcuin,
Aldebaran,
Alighieri
Amphion,
Andronicus,
Antinous,
Aquinas,
Arab,
Aral,
Arundel,
Athos,
Avon,
Aytoun,
Bajazet,
Balliol (college),
Balmoral

Czerny
Latin,
Laocoön,
Medici,
Mivart,
    (St. George),
Orion,
Paderewski
Pepys,
Proserpine,
Sienkiewicz,
Southey,
Thalia,
Tschaikowsky,
Volapük
Wagner,
Ygdrasil.

[1] The mark over the second syllable is called the diæresis. It indicates that each vowel is to be pronounced separately.

CHAPTER III

A REVIEW OF PUNCTUATION

Punctuation is a system of disjunctive marks by which the eye and ear are helped to understand the sense of what is written. It is desirable to regard the subject as governed to a great extent by a few principles of common sense. The present chapter reviews those matters of capitalization and punctuation which seem to give most trouble to secondary school students.

Capitals.

1. Of course all proper nouns should begin with capital letters, and so should adjectives derived from them: examples, *Russia, Russian, Jew, Jewish, Gentile, French, German.* But the word *christian* is not always capitalized, especially if it is used vaguely as a synonym for good, righteous, etc.

2. We capitalize the words *North, South, East, West,* when, because we mean parts of the country, we use the article *the* before them. Thus, " The extreme West favors free silver." But if we speak of direction merely, we do not capitalize: " Many

people took Horace Greeley's advice and went west." Capitalize sections of the country, but not points of the compass.

3. Names of the seasons are not capitalized. Thus, though we write *June, September,* we also write *spring, autumn.*

4. In the salutation of a letter, the word *Sir* is capitalized, but not the preceding adjective unless that begins the salutation. Thus: "My dear Sir." So in the leave-taking only the first word receives a capital. Thus· "Yours very truly."

5. One valuable device is the use of the capital to introduce the semblance of a quotation, or what might be called a rhetorical quotation. Note: "I should answer, No." Here the quotation *No* is merely rhetorical, or pretended, not real. Or this· "Let me give you a short rule for success: Trust in God and keep your powder dry." Or this, from Longfellow: "Perhaps the greatest lesson which the lives of literary men teach us is told in a single word: Wait!"

6. In titles of books, essays, etc., the important words are capitalized. Thus: "My theme-title to-day was, A Description of a Person."

7. Names of Deity begin with a capital, and many persons prefer to capitalize adjectives referring directly to Deity. Thus: "We crave Thy grace." But this habit should not be carried so far as the capitalization of words like *divine, omnis-*

cient, when these are not applied to Deity. Rather:
" His goodness was divine."

Written Exercise. — Copy the following, capitalizing where necessary : —

1. After going south last spring I understood better than before what is meant by the new south. The southerners have taken to manufacturing; the cotton is no longer all shipped away. Wealth has multiplied. Immigration has increased — the french are not the only foreigners now. There are colleges and even universities, that compare favorably with those of the north. Are the people wide-awake and ambitious ? I answer, yes.

The Reasons for Punctuation. — In early days manuscripts were written " solid," thus : —

MANUSCRIPTSWEREWRITTENSOLID.

It was found that both eye and ear demanded spaces and punctuation. The reader's train of thought goes straight ahead from word to word until the punctuation mark warns it that there is danger of misunderstanding if it does not pause. The mark shows that the words which precede it are to be understood mentally as a group, and to be read orally as a group. If the thought is kept in mind that a punctuation mark is a sort of danger signal, many of the difficulties of the subject vanish. " Henry rose, and I with him laughed at the story we had heard." If that comma be omitted between *rose* and *and,* what happens ?

The Comma.

1. The comma, even more than other points, shows what the meaning of the sentence is; it should set off the parts of the thought. Nothing is easier than to spoil a minor unit of thought by breaking it in two with a comma. So far as may be, the modified subject of a sentence should not be cut into by a comma; neither should the modified predicate; nor should a subject and its predicate be separated any oftener by commas than is necessary. The following passage, written by a lad of fifteen from dictation, shows the minor units of thought divided by too many commas : —

The mean appearance of the houses, in old Boston, was, to some extent, relieved by the rich display, of painted, and sculptured signs, which adorned the front of taverns, and stores. . . . They served sometimes, as advertisements of the business, sometimes merely as designations, of the shops which were indicated popularly, and, in the newspapers, by their signs.

If this passage be read aloud, a pause being made wherever a comma is placed, it will sound unnatural, disconnected. Revised, it will read somewhat as follows : —

The mean appearance of the houses in old Boston was, to some extent, relieved by the rich display of painted and sculptured signs which adorned the front of taverns and stores. . . . They served sometimes as advertisements of the business, sometimes merely as designations of the shops, which were indicated popularly and in the newspapers by their signs.

2. Commas are used to set off matter that is parenthetical, but not sufficiently so as to need parentheses or dashes. Such words as *therefore* are not usually to be considered as parenthetical. A parenthetical group of words is not to be broken into unnecessarily by a comma. Incorrect form: "The squire remarked, as all we who live here, in Smithboro, know, that, so far as the people who lived over there, in Edinburgh, are concerned, we are as happy as they." Correct form: "The squire remarked, as all we who live here in Smithboro' know, that so far as the people who live over there in Edinburgh are concerned, we are as happy as they."

3. Vocative words, that is, words used in direct address, are set off by commas. "Come, men, let's go!" "Well, sir, how now?" It is curious that in the expressions "Yes, sir," "No, sir," in pronouncing which we do not pause before "*sir*," we still place a comma here. Probably no rule of punctuation is more neglected than this of vocative words. Something like this usage is the placing of a comma after the expletive *Now*. Thus: "Now, I think that the case is a little different."

4. (*a*) Words or phrases forming a series are separated by commas when conjunctions are omitted; and the comma is used between the last two members of the series, conjunction or no conjunction. Thus · " Burns, Barnes of Dorsetshire, and Riley are poets of the people." If the last comma were omitted, we should seem not to be considering each man separately. Exceptions: " little old man," " fine fat hen," etc.

(*b*) A rapid series of independent propositions, very closely related in sense, may be punctuated by commas. Thus: " I came, I saw, I conquered." This is the only structure in which an independent statement, not introduced by a conjunction, is ever pointed with the comma. If there is any doubt whether or not the series is rapid enough to admit commas, semicolons should be used instead.

5. Relative clauses not restrictive [1] are set off by commas. This is a rather important rule. If I say, " The moon, which, as everybody is aware, goes round the earth, is cold," the *which* clause does not so restrict or define the word " moon " that it is necessary to our understanding what is meant by " the moon "; the relative clause can be picked out bodily, and the sentence will still be intelligible. " The moon is cold," is clear enough to people who

---

[1] Such may be called logically co-ordinate, though grammatically dependent. The restrictive relative clause may be called the necessary relative clause ; the non-restrictive may be called the unnecessary or additional relative clause.

live on the earth. They understand that the earth's moon is meant. But suppose I say, "The moon which goes round the earth is smaller than one of Jupiter's moons"; now the relative clause identifies, restricts the word "moon" — tells what moon is meant. The clause forms an integral part of the subject. It is no longer the moon merely, a thing that everybody knows about; it is one particular moon : the-moon-which-goes-round-the-earth. Occasionally such a clause can be identified by *that*, for many writers save this relative for restrictive clauses.

Written Exercise. — Copy and punctuate the following sentences, all of which, except the first are from Robert Louis Stevenson. Defend orally your pointing : —

1. There goes President Harper who is so much interested in everything that interests students.

2. Marquis I said if you take another step I fire upon you.

3. In the midst of these imagine that natural clumsy unintelligent and mirthful animal John.

4. The terms and spirit in which he spoke of his political beliefs were in our eyes suited to religious beliefs and *vice versa.*

5. Oh yes I dare say said John.

6. Moy pronounced Moÿ was a pleasant little village.

7. We were in a large bare apartment adorned with two allegorical prints of music and painting and a copy of the law against public drunkenness

8. Now what I like so much in France is the clear unflinching recognition by everybody of his own luck

9. If it ever be a good thing to take such despondency to heart the Miserere is the right music and a cathedral a fit scene

10. But the sun was already down the air was chill and we had scarcely a dry stitch between the pair of us

11. The inn to which we had been recommended at Quartes was full.

12. Mme. Gilliard set herself to waken the boy who had come far that day and was peevish and dazzled by the light.

13. Do you remember the Frenchman who was put down at Waterloo Station

14. The children who played together to-day by the Sambre and Oise canal each at his own father's threshold when and where might they next meet

15. I began with a remark upon their dog which had somewhat the look of a pointer

16. The only buildings that had any interest for us were the hotel and the café

17. Not long after the drums had passed the café [we] began to grow sleepy and set out for the hotel which was only a door or two away

The Semicolon.

1. The semicolon is a kind of weak full-stop, *i.e.* period. Nearly always it separates clauses that are grammatically able to get along without each other, but that are closely related in sense. So rare indeed are the cases in which the semicolon may be used with a dependent clause, that a high school student may properly ignore them. *For the present, avoid using the semicolon to point a dependent clause.*

2. Sometimes the semicolon punctuates a series of mere phrases. This occurs if some particular emphasis is desired for them, or if they are too long to be set off by commas. Example : —

An enormous smoke-stack blocks my view ; built of brick, and massive ; blue in the cold winter mist ; glowing like a pillar of fire as soon as the sunlight reaches it ; the most changing, the most stable, thing is this landscape.

Oral Exercise. — Which statements in the following sentences are independent ? which dependent ? (It need hardly be suggested that the necessity of understanding a subject or a predicate does not make a statement dependent.)

1. If the sky falls, we shall catch larks.
2. Faults are thick, where love is thin.
3. Happy is he that is happy in his children.
4. Histories make men wise ; poets, witty ; the

mathematics, subtile; natural philosophy, deep; morals, grave; logic and rhetoric, able to contend.

5. O, there be players that I have seen play, — and heard others praise, and that highly — not to speak it profanely, that neither having the accent of Christians, nor the gait of Christian, pagan, nor man, have so strutted and bellowed, that I have thought some of nature's journeymen had made men, and not made them well, they imitated humanity so abominably. — *Hamlet*, Act III. Sc. 2.

The following sentences were written by a pupil in the first year of the high school. If there are mistakes in punctuation, explain what principle is violated: —

1. When the time came to retire; my uncle was shown to the tower-room.

2. A short time afterward,when he was travelling through Normandy; he came to an old castle standing in the midst of a park.

3. The postilion was ordered to drive to the castle; where my uncle received a welcome from the little Marquis.

4. This seemed the very night for ghosts; with the wind howling outside and whistling through the ill-fitting casement.

The Colon.

1. The colon is usually a mark of specification. Thus, "The old idea of education was simple:

reading, writing, arithmetic." A fine distinction of logic can be shown by using it : a general statement may be followed by a colon, after which the details that explain the statement may be given. In the following sentence the colon *specifies* what is meant by fine character. " He was a fellow of fine character : brave, honorable, free from false pretense." Usually the colon separates clauses that are logically, if not grammatically, in *apposition* with each other.

2. The colon introduces a formal or long, the comma an informal or short, quotation. " He answered, ' I will work while the day lasts.' " " The Declaration of Independence begins as follows : ' When, in the course of human events.' "

The Dash.

1. The dash shows a sudden break in the thought. Thus · " We were hurrying onward — but first let me tell what happened before that."

2. The dash sometimes precedes a *summing up*. Here it usually follows a comma, since the members of the series are set off by commas: "Chaucer, Shakespeare, Wordsworth, — very many of our great poets indeed, were at home in the country." Sometimes the dash is used when there is no real summing up, but an appositive phrase is added, as a further explanation. For an example, see the last sentence of the next paragraph, — and this sentence also.

3. The dash, like the comma, is often used to set off a parenthetical expression. (See 2, under the comma.) Examples: " His father — that iron gentleman — had long ago dethroned himself." " He was a man — the reader must already have perceived — of easy, not to say familiar, manners." Note that in these examples no commas are used with the dashes, because if the parenthetical words were lifted out, the sentence would close up without punctuation. But suppose the sentence were such that it could not close up without punctuation ; then the comma would be needed. The comma in " His father being angry, he felt afraid," remains when the parenthesis is inserted: " His father being angry, — that iron gentleman, — he felt afraid." Note that in such a case a second comma is used, — with the second dash.

Written Exercise. — Copy and punctuate the following sentences from Stevenson. In the first is there not a choice of punctuation after " difficulties " ?

1. All the way down we had our fill of difficulties sometimes it was a wear which could be shot sometimes one so shallow and full of stakes that we must withdraw the boats from the water and carry them round

2. But this is a fashion I love to kiss the hand or wave a handkerchief to people I shall never see

again to play with possibility and knock in a peg for fancy to hang upon

3. You see what it is to be a gentleman I beg your pardon what it is to be a pedler.

4. Centralization said he but the landlord was at his throat in a minute

5. There should be some myth but if there is I know it not founded on the shivering of the reeds there are not many things in nature more striking to man's eye

6. " The fire should have been here at this side " explained the husband " then one might have a writing table in the middle books and " comprehensively [1] " all it would be quite coquettish *ça serait tout-à-fait coquet.*"

Quotation Marks.

1. Marks of quotation, or, as the English call them, inverted commas, are placed around direct quotations. Many students neglect a part of this little duty: they fail to mark *the end* of the quotation.

2. A quotation within a quotation stands between single commas. Thus· " We were gathered on shore, watching the schooner. Gray spoke up: ' She's certainly going down, and we must let the saving station know it. Maybe the patrol has

[1] *Comprehensively* is Mr. Stevenson's word — not the *husband's;* it is inserted to show the way in which, probably with a vague gesture, the husband said *all.*

D

already seen her; I saw a sailor walking on the beach not long since, and singing, "Yeave ho, my lads, the wind blows free."'" Note that when there is a quotation *within the second quotation*, it receives the double marks.

3. Sometimes a quotation is given in substance, with no attempt at accuracy; to show this fact it is quoted in single commas. Thus: 'A foolish consistency frightens little minds.' This is the substance of Emerson's remark, "A foolish consistency is the bugbear of little minds."

Theme — Write a dialogue a page or two long. Show the change from speaker to speaker by the use of quotation marks and paragraphing. Each reply of each interlocutor, with its word or two of introduction, if such there be, should go by itself as a paragraph. Choose your own topic; or take one of these, changing the wording: (1) Smith tries to make Brown see the difference between relative clauses restrictive and those merely coördinate. (2) Two girls lament the difficulties of punctuation. (3) Two lads [or, men] talk politics. Do not begin each speech as in Shakespeare each is begun — with the speaker's name. Refer occasionally to the speakers, if you please, *e.g.*, "'Not by any means,' responded Bangs, rather tartly"; but do not hesitate to let most of the speeches stand without comment. Punctuate the dialogue carefully, as you write. Then revise it carefully for punctuation.

Brackets. — Brackets indicate that the included matter is inserted by another person than the original author; that is, by a person who is quoting or editing the passage. Thus: " He [Goethe] tells us that character is developed in the busy world though intellect is developed in solitude."

The Exclamation Point.

1. There is a tendency to punctuate with the period sentences that are really exclamatory; it is better to use the exclamation point. Thus: " I am so delighted to see you ! "

It is better still to avoid an excess of exclamatory sentences, however correctly punctuated.

2. The word *oh!* should be followed by an exclamation point or by a comma. This is not the word *O,* which is used in direct address —

> " O thou that rollest above,
>   Round as the shield of my fathers,"

and to express a wish:

> " O that I had wings like a dove."

3. The exclamation point may stand in the midst of a sentence, at the end of a clause. The mark is then not followed by a capital letter. Thus: " Is it possible ! is it credible ! " exclaimed the Bishop.

The Interrogation Point.

1. Placed in parentheses the interrogation point questions the accuracy of a statement. Ex.: " It is in New York (?) that the largest number of exiled Russians is found."

2. Like the exclamation mark, the question mark may stand at the end of a clause, before a small letter. Thus: " Do you believe it ? was the way he greeted me as I finished reading the letter." Or, " Shall we lie here inactive ? Shall we plan nothing ? attempt nothing ? do nothing ? "

Written Exercise. — Copy and punctuate the following sentences from Stevenson : —

1. Such a dinner as we were going to eat such beds as we were to sleep in

2. Where were the boating men of Belgium where the judge and his good wines and where the graces of Origny

3. Come back again she cried and all the hills echoed her

4. All the gold had withered out of the sky and the balloon had disappeared whither I ask myself ; caught up into the seventh heaven or come safely to land somewhere in that blue uneven distance into which the roadway dipped and melted before our eyes

Italics.

1. A good rule for italics is to shun them — that is, not to use them freely to denote emphasis.

Emphasis can be secured by some other means · for instance, by putting the emphatic word near the beginning of the sentence. Thus: " It was such a very *fine* thing to spin along over the ice " becomes, " A fine thing it was, to spin along over the ice."

2. Use italics to show that a word is foreign. Thus · " Sophronia likes to interlard her English with such fine phrases as *en passant, fin .de siècle,* and *al ;fresco.*"

3. It is usual to italicize single words if they are specified, — spoken of as words. Thus: " A good many words that pass muster with most people are not really in good use; for example, *burglarize.*"

The Apostrophe.

1. One use of the apostrophe is to mark the plural of single letters, or figures. Ex.: Distinguish between your 8's and 3's; dot your *i's* and cross your *t's.*

2. The commoner use of the apostrophe is to mark the possessive case. There is however no apostrophe in the word *its,* which is considered an adjective, not a personal, pronoun.

Asterisks. — A row of asterisks is used to show an omission. Thus, if a writer were quoting, and wished to skip a page or two, he would insert this sign * * * * But if he omitted only a few words, he would rather use " leaders "; thus . . . .

Oral Exercise, in Review. — Read this passage over carefully, and listen to the reading of it aloud by some member of the class or by the instructor. Then explain how it should be punctuated.

Mr. Higginbotham Mr. Higginbotham tell us the particulars about old Mr. Higginbotham bawled the mob what is the coroner's verdict are the murderers apprehended is Mr. Higginbotham's· niece come out of her fainting fits Mr. Higginbotham Mr. Higginbotham

The coachman said not a word except to swear awfully at the ostler for not bringing him a fresh team of horses the lawyer inside had generally his wits about him even when asleep the first thing he did after learning the cause of the excitement was to produce a large red pocket-book meantime Dominicus Pike being an extremely polite young man and also suspecting that a female tongue would tell the story as glibly as a lawyer's had handed the lady out of the coach she was a fine smart girl now wide awake and bright as a button and had such a sweet pretty mouth that Dominicus would almost as lieves have heard a love tale from it as a tale of murder

Gentleman and ladies said the lawyer to the shopkeepers the mill men and the factory girls I can assure you that some unaccountable mistake or more probably a wilful falsehood maliciously contrived to injure Mr Higginbotham's credit has excited this singular uproar we passed through Kimballton at three o'clock this morning and most certainly should have been informed of the murder had any been perpetrated but I have proof nearly as strong as Mr. Higginbotham's own oral testimony in the negative here is a note relating to a suit of his in the Connecticut courts which was delivered me from that gentleman himself I find it dated at ten o'clock last evening

So saying the lawyer exhibited the date and signature of the note which irrefragably proved either that this perverse Mr. Higginbotham was alive when he wrote it or as some deemed the more probable case of two doubtful ones that he was so absorbed in worldly business as to continue to transact it even after his death but unexpected evidence was forthcoming the young lady after listening to the pedlers explanation merely seized a moment to smooth her gown and put her curls in order, and then appeared at the tavern-door making a modest signal to be heard

Good people said she I am Mr. Higginbotham's niece

Written Exercise, in Review. — Copy, punctuate, and capitalize the following, from Charles Lamb :

And first let us remember as first in importance in our childish eyes the young men as they almost were who under the denomination of *Grecians* were

waiting the expiration of the period when they
should be sent at the charges of the Hospital to
one or other of our Universities but more frequently to Cambridge these youths from their
superior acquirements their superior age and stat-
ure and the fewness of their numbers for seldom
above two or three at a time were inaugurated into
that high order drew the eyes of all and especially
of the younger boys into a reverent observance and
admiration how tall they used to seem to us how
stately would they pace along the cloisters while
the play of the lesser boys was absolutely suspended
or its boisterousness at least allayed at their presence not that they ever beat or struck the boys that
would have been to have demeaned [1] themselves the
dignity of their persons alone insured them all respect the task of blows, or corporal chastisement
they left to the common monitors or heads of wards
who it must be confessed in our time had rather
too much license allowed them to oppress and misuse their inferiors and the interference of the
Grecian who may be considered as the spiritual
power was not unfrequently called for to mitigate
by its mediation the heavy unrelenting arm of this
temporal power or monitor in fine the Grecians
were the solemn Muftis of the school œras [2] were
computed from their time it used to be said such

[1] Demean = behave. What word would be better here?
[2] A quaint way of spelling *eras*.

or such a thing was done when S —— or T ——
was Grecian.

Common Abbreviations.

The following list of abbreviations should be learned
Latin words and all.

A. B., *Artium Baccalaureus.* Bachelor of Arts. In England, B. A.

A. D., *Anno Domini.* In the Year of our Lord.

AD. LIB., or *ad. lib., Ad libitum.* At pleasure.

ÆT., *Ætatis.* Of age ; aged.

A. M., *Ante Meridiem.* Before noon.

A. M., *Artium Magister.* Master of Arts. In England,
M. A.

A. U. C., *Anno Urbis Conditæ.* In the year from the Building of the City (Rome).

D. C. L. Doctor of Civil Law.

D. D., *Divinitatis Doctor.* Doctor of Divinity.

D. D. S. Doctor of Dental Surgery.

Do., *Ditto.* The same.

E. E. Errors excepted. (Used in book-keeping.)

E. O. E. Errors and omissions excepted.

E. G., or *e. g., Exempli gratia.* For example.

ETC., or &c., *Et cœtera.* And so forth ; literally, And
others.

F. R. S. Fellow of the Royal Society.

H. M. His *or* Her Majesty.

H. M. S. His *or* Her Majesty's Ship *or* Service.

H. R. H. His *or* Her Royal Highness.

IBID., *Ibidem.* In the same place. Used in quoting several
selections from one book, or making several references to
one source.

I. E., or *i. e., Id est.* That is. In reading aloud, one gives
the English words only.

I. H. S., sometimes explained as *Iesus Hominum Salvator.*
Jesus the Saviour of Men. More properly, this abbrevia-

tion merely means "Jesus." It is made up of the first three letters of the Greek word for Jesus — IHΣOΤΣ. The H, in I. H. S., is really the Greek letter êta, from which we get our capital E.

I. N. R. I., *Iesus Nazarenus Rex Iudæorum.* Jesus of Nazareth, King of the Jews.

L. H. D., *Litterarum Humanarum Docto*r. Doctor of Humane *L*etters.

LL. D., *Legum Doctor.* Doctor of *L*aws.

M., *Meridies.* Mid-day.

M. A. Master of Arts.

M. D., *Medicinæ Docto*r. Doctor of Medicine.

Messrs. Gentlemen. (French, *Messieurs.*)

Mme. Madame.

Mlle. Mademoiselle.

MS., or Ms. Manuscript. MSS. Manuscripts.

N. B., *Nota bene.* Mark well, or take notice.

N. S. New Style (after 1752).

Ob., O*biit.* He *or* she died.

O. S. Old Style (previous to 1752).

Ph. D., *Philosophiæ Doctor.* Doctor of Philosophy.

Pp. Pages.

P. P. C., *Pour prendre congé.* To take leave. This is not an abbreviation for the English words : Paid parting call.

Pro tem., *Pro tempore.* For the time being.

Prox., *Proximo.* Next, *or* the next month.

Q. E. D., *Quod erat demonstrandum.* Which was to be demonstrated.

R. S. V. P., or R. s. v. p., *Répondez, s'il vous plaît.* Answer, if you please.

Viz., or viz., *Videlicet.* Namely, to wit. *Videlicet* has etymologically about the force of "You see," or "It can be seen."

Vs., *Versus.* Against.

CHAPTER IV

GRAMMATICAL PHASES OF WRITING ENGLISH

The present chapter reviews only those grammatical principles that are sometimes violated by students who have had a year of formal grammar.

Clearness. — If composition is the art of communicating one's ideas in words, it is certain that clearness is the first requisite of good writing. Clearness, perfect intelligibility, is secured by means innumerable. One secret however of being clear is to regard grammatical usages. If a man is to be understood exactly, he must be grammatical. No one is excepted. "Grammar," said Molière, "knows how to lord it even over kings."

Ambiguity. — When an expression is open to two interpretations, it is said to be ambiguous. In the sentence, "He is a fair man," *fair* is an ambiguous word. In the sentence, "He was arrested by two officers, who were about to board a West Madison street car, in possession of a large amount of stolen property," the phrase *in possession*, etc., holds an ambiguous position. Grammatical errors often produce this fault.

Solecisms. — Infringements of grammatical rules are called *solecisms*.[1] Never losing sight of the fact that writing English is largely the art of telling some one else just what one means, let us note a few solecisms that hinder a writer from giving his exact meaning.

Coherence by placing Modifiers rightly. — I. The rhetorics are fond of quoting droll sentences in which, from being wrongly placed, ideas fail to *cohere*, stick together. A favorite sentence is that from an epitaph in an Ulster churchyard: "Erected to the memory of John Phillips, accidently shot, as a mark of affection by his brother." Mr. Bardeen ("Sentence-Making") quotes the following, which sounds like a manufactured joke, but is nevertheless to the point. "Is there a gentleman with one eye named Walker in the club?" "I don't know; what was the name of his other eye?" Another much quoted and startling sentence reads thus· "In one evening I counted twenty-seven meteors sitting on my back piazza." Remedy the incoherence of these sentences. *Put close together on the paper ideas that belong close together in the mind.* Do not let adverbs and modifying clauses stray from the thought to which they belong.

[1] *Solecism* is Greek in origin. The Athenian colonists of Soli in Asia Minor spoke Greek so badly that the Attic Greeks came to refer to an error in grammar (or in pronunciation) as *soloikismós*, whence our word.

Oral Exercise. — The order of words in the following sentences should so be changed as to increase the logical coherence of the thoughts.

1. The tops of the French ships were filled with riflemen, like those of the enemy's ships.

2. The killing by Orlando, of the wrestler, was indirectly due to a plot against his brother, which Oliver invented.

3. I hardly ever remember to have heard such music.

4. I never remember to have seen him. [Here it is better to recast the sentence than to change the position of *never*.]

5. The lad managed a bronco pony, very vicious and dangerous, when only thirteen.

6. Wanted, a hostler to take care of a horse, of a religious turn of mind.

7. After a brief rest Blondin set out again with "Tom Sayers," and accomplished the feat he had undertaken without a hitch.

This week will see the last times of "The Rogue's Comedy," as next season Mr. Willard will play the new play of Henry Arthur Jones entitled "The Physician" exclusively.

II. *Only*, and *not only*, usually belong directly before the word modified.

Oral Exercise. — Insert *only* in the proper blank.

1. Browning —— wrote —— a few poems for boys.

2. She —— breathed —— the name; but we heard it.

3. We —— received his letter, —— this morning.

4. He —— gave —— five cents —— to the church.

III. Avoid the Janus-clause; the Janus-phrase; the Janus-adverb or adjective. The Latin god Janus had two faces, one looking back, the other ahead. Avoid putting a modifier where it becomes double-faced, — where it may be taken either with the preceding idea or with the following idea.

Oral Exercise. — So change the position of the double-faced modifiers that their allegiance will be known.

1. There is no doubt that Milton gave Dryden permission to paraphrase Paradise Lost; Dryden did imitate Milton as a matter of fact not very cleverly.

2. There can be no doubt that he quarrelled, — that he fought indeed vigorously. He reappeared at least with a black eye.

3. She will sing in any case charmingly; her training has been admirable.

4. As Hazlitt says, in his book of English proverbs, where no fault is, there needs no pardon.

IV. Avoid putting an adverb between the parts of an infinitive, — between the *to* and the verb. Some reputable writers approve this construction; still, the better order is to place the modifier before or after the whole infinitive. "Clearly to see," or "To see clearly," is better than "To clearly see." This error is called the *cleft infinitive.*

Concord of Subject and Predicate.

1. A collective noun takes a singular verb if the group of objects is thought of as a whole · "The United States is coining gold and silver." The collective noun takes a plural verb if each separate member of the group is thought of: "The United States are firmly bound together in one union."

2. When two subject nouns are so closely related in thought that they seem to mean one thing, the verb is in the singular: "His courage and bravery is well approved."

3. In writing a long sentence, glance back at the number of the subject before you write the verb. A plural near the verb often leads one to forget that the subject is singular. Thus · "The great number of the crows that settle nightly in the grove and fill the air with their cries, makes [not *make*] the place a bedlam."

4. When a singular subject precedes a parenthetical phrase, the former reaches over the head of the latter, and makes the verb singular. This rule holds even when the parenthesis is introduced by *with.* Thus: "Napoleon, with all his army, was on the march."

5. *Either, neither,* when used as distributive conjunctions, take a singular verb. Mr. Carpenter[1] gives this instance of the error: "Neither Senators Dawes nor Hoar were in their seats to-day." How shall the sentence be changed to distribute the senators properly?

6. If two subjects connected by *either — or,* etc., differ in person, it is possible to make the verb agree with the subject nearest; as "Neither she nor you are to blame in this; either I or he is to blame." But this construction is awkward. Avoid the difference in person, or else say, "Neither she is to blame, nor are you; either he is to blame, or I am."

7. *Each, every, either, neither,* when used as pronouns, always take a singular verb. "Each of us knows; neither of us is ignorant."

8. *None* takes either a singular or a plural verb. It is originally *no one,* and many careful writers prefer to keep the singular with it.

Concord of Adjective (or Participle) and Noun.

1. There is an old phrase, *these kind,* which, though permitted a century ago, was essentially ungrammatical, and is not allowed to-day. Say *this kind, that kind,* etc.

2. (*a*) Every participle, like every adjective, must agree with its noun in person and number.

[1] *Advanced Exercises,* p. 85.

But furthermore, every participle has an indisputable right to have something to agree with. Too often the poor word is left dangling in mid air. *Shun the unrelated participle and the misrelated participle.* The best of us are only too prone to such slips as this: "Coming up stairs, it was seen that the great window fell," instead of, "Coming up stairs, we saw the great window fall." Or this: "Coming up stairs, the window fell on him," where the *coming* may belong to the *window* or to the *him.* In the first of the two incorrect sentences the participle is unrelated; in the second it is misrelated, or at least ambiguously related.

(*b*) Care should be taken not to use a participle when a verbal noun in *ing* is needed. "The fact of *Poe being* intemperate should not blind us to the fact of his genius," is wrong for "The fact of *Poe's being* intemperate," etc.

3. Particularly avoid a singular adjective with a plural noun, in such expressions as, "A long way" [not *ways*]. Note here that *sidewise,* not *sideways,* is correct.

Concord of Pronoun and Antecedent.

1. It should be remembered that every singular antecedent takes a singular pronoun. "Everybody came forward and laid *his* contribution on the table" — not "*their* contribution."

2. Before writing the verb of a relative clause,

E

think whether the antecedent is singular or plural. "Her voice is one of the sweetest that have [not *has*] been heard in this town."

3. When a number of persons, men and women, are spoken of distributively, the pronouns *he* and *his* are proper forms of reference — not *their*, not *his or her* "The audience rose and each person waved *his* applause" would be correct, even if there were ten ladies to each man. The *he* or *his* may here be called the *neutral* pronoun. What pronouns should fill the blanks in the following sentence? "Let every man and woman who would like to join our picnic betake —— to the pier at three o'clock, and give —— no anxiety about —— lunch; —— will find plenty of sandwiches and cake and coffee on the picnic-boat."

Such expressions as "every man and woman" are however undesirable whenever the neutral pronoun is to be used. A neutral antecedent, like *every person, everybody, every one,* is preferable.

4. When the indefinite pronoun *one* is used, there is often ambiguity in referring to it later by *he, his,* etc. Repeat the *one.* Thus, "One does not always know one's own mind." Better still, use an expression like the indefinite *you,* or, *a person,* which has its own representative among the pronouns. Thus, "A person doesn't always know his own mind.'

5. Use sparingly, if at all, the Latin construction

— *which* '*fact, which idea,* etc. Say rather, *a* '*fact which,* etc. *E.g.* " He was slightly deaf, *a misfortune which* he bore without whimpering."

6. Avoid the Latin construction that makes *which* refer to the idea of a whole clause; it is a clumsy fashion. Example, " He said that he always doted on Shakespeare — *which* I, for one, didn't believe, because I know the fellow." There is nothing here for *which* to tie to; it is a relative without anything to which to relate. Rather a better way is to discard the relative clause, substituting *and* with a demonstrative. Thus, " He bowed politely, *which* set us all at ease," becomes, " He bowed politely, *and this* set us all at ease." The *this* is allowed by our idiom to refer to the clause, though the construction is still vague. It is best to hunt up a good synonym for the idea of the preceding clause: " He bowed politely, and this *courtesy* set us all at ease." But it is not necessary to discard the relative clause. A little ingenuity will enable one to find and insert just before the relative an appositive to the clause. Into each of the following sentences slip an appropriate appositive chosen from the following list: *a* '*fact, an idea, a task, a statement, an assertion, a notion, an excuse, a* '*fancy, a belief, a hyperbole, a prevarication, a remedy.*

(*a*) Mr. Ignatius Donnelly thinks that Bacon wrote Shakespeare, —— which ought not to bother the student who likes Romeo and Juliet.

(*b*) Mame told father that there were a thousand cats in the back yard, —— which, according to father, meant our cat and another.

(*c*) He has undertaken to learn two hard lessons in one hour, —— which will probably prove too much for the lad.

(*d*) He proposes to cut the hand off, —— which seems rather cruel.

Concord of Cases.

Subject and complement of an intransitive verb agree in case.

1. The complement of an intransitive verb in a finite mode is in the nominative case. "It's I" [not *me*] "I am he." "I thought it was he."

2. If the subject of an infinitive is in the objective case, the complement is in the same case. "I thought it to be him" [not *he*]. But, "It was thought to be he."

Concord of Tenses.

1. In writing the verb of a subordinate clause, be sure that its tense shall show just what you wish it to show — whether the *same* time as that of the principal verb, or *earlier* time, or *later* time. For example: —

The same time. — "He did not think himself to be much of a poet."

Earlier time. — "He did not think that he had been much of a poet." "He was sorry not to have been much of a poet." "Yesterday, when John spoke of the matter, I should have liked to have had some experience that I might have used in advising him."

Later time. — "I wanted to go" [not *to have gone*]. "I had intended to go." "I should have liked to go."

Oral Exercise. — Correct the errors in concord of tenses, explaining each emendation.

1. Where did you say St. Peter's was?

2. Is it warm out of doors? I should say it was.

3. I fully intended to have met you at the concert.

Government.

1. "He invited him and *I*," is not an unheard-of blunder. People often needlessly shrink from saying a correct sentence like this — "He invited him and me" — and will even insert the full names of *him* and *me* rather than out with the right case of the pronoun.

2. In asking a question, think whether *who* or *whom* is required. "*Whom* did you see?" but, "*Who* was it that you saw?"

3. *Let* governs the objective case, quite as any other active verb "Let John and me go."

4. An error often occurs in the case of the relative after a verb of saying, thinking, telling, and the like. "Franklin's Autobiography is the

work of a man *whom* I should think, would be
known to every American." The *whom* is wrong
for *who*. Had the writer set off " I should think "
by commas, he would have seen the mistake.

5. How should the following newspaper sentence be corrected ? " He stated that the offering
was $101,500, an amount upon which he would
stake his honor would all be paid up."

On the Reference of Pronouns.

1. In the use of pronouns one cannot be too careful that each refers to the right person. " Farmer
Jones called on his neighbor and told him that
his cows were in his pasture," leaves us in doubt
whether Farmer Jones came to make a complaint
or an apology. How should the sentence be constructed to remove the ambiguity ? The following
delicious error has been much quoted : " If fresh
milk does not seem to agree with the child, boil
it." How change the sentence to save the child's
life ?

2. Sometimes a demonstrative can be used to
better advantage than a personal pronoun. "They
lent us their horses for the afternoon and these
[not *they*] took us a long way out into the country."

3. Sometimes it is better to repeat the antecedent, varying it by simple synonyms, than to use
any pronoun. Not, " He gave him his word of

honor, that whenever he should see his brother in London, he would do all for him that he ought to do for an old comrade's brother." Rather thus· " He gave his friend his word of honor, that whenever he should see the latter's brother in London, he would do for the boy all that a man ought to do for the brother of an old comrade."

4. Acquire a habit of writing, " It is he," or " It's he," instead of " He is the one." This latter phrase is permissible in colloquial speech, where its clumsiness is not much felt. The correct expression may sometimes seem over-precise. But a person of tact ought to be able to speak correctly without seeming affected.

Conjunctions and Prepositions.

1. Shall we say " as large as," " not as large as," etc.? The first expression is right. But after a negative, use *so* for a correlative to *as :* " not *so* large as."

2. In general be careful not to omit necessary conjunctions. What should be supplied in the following sentence ? and how should the order be changed? " Henty is better known but not so interesting to older boys as Stevenson."

3. *And which, and who,* etc., are wrong for *which, who,* etc., when no relative has previously been used. Correct the following: " Irving, the historian, and whom we honor as our first writer of prose tales, is a prime favorite of us all."

4. *Like* is not a conjunction. It is incorrect to say, "Do like I do" This wrong use of *like* is habitual in many parts of our country, and a native of any one of these districts has to watch himself narrowly to acquire the habit of using *as* for *like*. It is, however, correct enough to say, "She talks *like him*." Here *like* is an adjective governing what was the dative case, and the phrase *like him* has the value of an adverb.

5. *Different to* is wrong for *different from*. This error, though rarely to be found in America, is habitual in England. The commoner American error is *different than*. This mistake frequently occurs when the comparative degree has previously been used. *E.g.* "This last kind of apple is different and sweeter than the first." The better form is: "This last kind of apple is different from the first, and sweeter." *Do not split the particles*, by saying, "This kind of apple is different from and sweeter than the first."

Adverb or Adjective?

1. There is a group of words — verbs of sensation and the like, *look sound, feel, smell, taste, appear, seem* — which take an adjective to complete their meaning. "She looks *sweet*," "It tastes *sweet*," "She *seems* happy," are common and correct ways of speaking. *Notice that here something of the same idea can be given by saying, "She is*

sweet," "It *is* sweet," "She *is* happy." The *sweet* idea or the *happy* idea describes the subject, the person, not the verb. Of course, one might write a sentence in which the *sweet* idea would tell the way a given act was done. "She looked sweetly" would imply that she was gazing sweetly at something or somebody.

But here must be noted an exception or two. (*a*) The word *bad* has two senses: moral badness and badness that is not moral — badness of health for instance. If I say "I feel bad," the bad seems to mean moral badness: *i.e.* "I *am* bad." It is therefore permissible to break the rule and apply *badly* to physical feeling. "I feel badly" is a common expression for "I feel sick"; and by the exception to the rule is correct. Which is better ın the following sentence — *bad* or *badly?* "It sounds —— to hear a young man swear." (*b*) There are a few cases where the adverb is retained when the verb is not felt as acting "The report sounds well," certainly does not mean that the report is in good health; but it is certainly good English. Similarly we have· "She appears well in company."

It is to be kept in mind that *ill* and *well* are not always adverbs. They are often adjectives; and if one says "I feel ill," or "I feel well," one is using the adjective *ill* or the adjective *well.*

Oral Exercise. — Which of the italicized words is preferable in the following sentences? (*a*) "This old stern-wheel boat rides over the waves quite as *easy* (*easily*) as any propeller, if not *easier* (*more easily*)." (*b*) "This old chaise rides as *easy* (*easily*) as any modern one." (*c*) "An old shoe feels *easy* (*easily*)." (*d*) "As Billings read that passage it sounded *different* (*differently*) from the way in which the Colonel read it." (*e*) "Do you feel *good* (*well*) after your night's rest?" (*f*) "I've been to church and, for me, really feel *good* (*well*)." (*g*) "He voted *independently* (*independent*)." (*h*) "Home, sweet home" sounds *well* (*good*) to the ears of the American abroad.

Shall or Will. — Most Americans, like most Scotchmen, use the word *will* too frequently, to the neglect of *shall*.

Shall is from Old English *sceal* (skay'-al) and once meant *owe, be obliged*. It still may mean the same thing, when not used as a mere auxiliary. That is, *should* often means *ought*, which was once the past tense of *owe*. It still can mean "to be obliged." "You shall," "he shall," are expressions that imply obligation, imposed by the speaker. "I shall at last die" still has in it the idea of being compelled. But this phrase illustrates happily one way by which *shall* with the first person has come to be felt as a mere future.

Nearly always to-day *I shall* names a voluntary act; but the volition is usually not emphasized; the speaker has usually made up his mind before he says *I shall*, and the words simply foretell the future act. "I shall be there" incidentally announces the speaker's intention, but the chief thing it announces is that the speaker will *be there*. It is probably the future fact that is of interest to his friends. *Ordinarily, therefore,* shall *in the first person means futurity more than it means volition.*

Will is from *wilian* (wil'-yan), meaning *to wish, to will*. It frequently means that to-day, though in the second and third persons it is also used for the simple future. "I will" always implies volition. I will *implies either deliberate intention, distinct wish, or distinct willingness.* "I will go" means "I am determined to go," or, "I wish to go," or, "I am willing to go." Frequently such a phrase implies that there is opposition or an obstacle. "You will," "they will," usually lack the volitive idea; they simply foretell that which *you, they,* are about to do. Yet *you will, he will, they will* may still mean *you are determined*, etc., if applied to a being that has the power of choice. Here one has but to emphasize the *will*, and the old meaning is brought back. Thus: "He *will* persist in doing so, though all his friends deplore it."

Our first rule will accordingly be as follows: *To indicate mere futurity, use* shall *in the first person,*

will *in the second and third*.   Examples: " I shall
be glad to come.   You and the others will find me
on hand at the pier."   So far, so good.   But note that
this rule also applies when the speaker is made to
report his own words in indirect narrative.   " Abner *says* that he *shall* be glad to come, and that you
and the others *will* find him on hand at the pier."
Just so if the indirect discourse is in the *past*, and
it is still the speaker who reports his own words.
" Abner *said* that he *should* be glad to come, and
that you and the others *would* find him at the
pier."   All this seems sensible enough, for the
speaker is merely made to foretell his own future
act.   The rule is too often broken.   " Abner said
he was afraid he'd miss the boat."   Here the contraction *he'd* stands (as always) for *he would*, a
form that is wrong in this place for *he should*.

The same rule applies when the indirect narrative is merely implied; that is, when instead of
such a word as *say* we have *think*, or *fear*, or *believe*.   " Luke thinks he *shall* miss his boat," is
correct; so is, " Luke feared he *should* miss the
boat."

Suppose, now, it is no longer what Luke said about
his own future act, but what somebody else said
about it.   " Evarts remarked that Luke was ready
and *would* hurry to the pier; but Evarts feared that
Luke *would* miss the boat "   The *shall* gives place
naturally enough to *will*.   *After verbs of saying,*

thinking, telling, and the like, shall (*or* should) *is the proper auxiliary if the future act is foretold by the actor*

Now we are ready to ask how these words should be used in questions. A very simple rule is enough for most purposes: *In the second and third persons use in the question the form you expect in the answer.*

"Shall you be at the pier by three, Abner?" Abner replies, "I certainly shall." "Will you kindly bring my lunch with you? the cook has it ready." "I will, with great pleasure."

The rule holds when applied to indirect discourse. Thus: "Abner's aunt asked him whether he *should* be at the pier by three. Abner replied that he *should.* Then she wanted to know if he *would* kindly bring her lunch along; Abner promised that he *would.*"

If a question is put in the first person, *shall* often asks for instructions. "*Shall* I go?" But if mere information is asked, *shall* is still the form "*Shall* I be required to do all this?" "Yes, I fear you will." Briefly, then, *for a question in the first person always use* shall.

Oral Exercise. — Where blanks appear in the following sentences insert the right auxiliary. Correct any misuse of auxiliaries.

1. Sometimes an Irishman, sometimes a Frenchman, is credited with this remark· "I will be drowned; nobody shall help me."

2. I —— be delighted to see you with us.

3. I —— be obliged if you —— lend me your pencil.

4. The director thinks he —— be able to speak well of that student, if the boy —— need a good word.

5. —— you be content if you get to college?

6. —— I be permitted to say that you —— see him before anything is done?

7. Jim Hawkins was mortally afraid that he —— be killed by Long John Silver; and in turn Long John began to fear that Jim —— be the death of him.

8. —— you like some bread? [Here *should* is the right word; *to like* is a word of volition, and it does not need the volitive auxiliary *would.*]

9. —— you mind my asking where you bought that jersey?

10. His father insisted that he —— stick to the task; and the son afterwards seemed glad of the fact, and asked whether he —— do some more work of the same sort.

11. If we were better, we —— be happier.

12. In which sentence can a contraction of *he would* be used? (*a*) He said —— be glad to accept. (*b*) Luther declared —— go to a certain city, though there were as many devils there as tiles on the housetops.

13. —— I be asked to go? Yes, you will.

14. Of whom —— I be afraid?

Matters of Etymology.

1. Good usage recommends that we say "the schools of Chicago" rather than "Chicago's schools"; "the cause of the accident" rather than "the accident's cause." In other words, it recommends that we save the possessive in *'s* (or Saxon genitive) for living beings. For things, for abstract ideas, for cities — everything except beings — the possessive in *of* (or Norman genitive) is preferred. Thus we say, "Napoleon's hat," and "the rim of Napoleon's hat," instead of "Napoleon's hat's rim." The newspapers, perhaps to save space, have fallen into the habit of talking about "Chicago's interests," "Evanston's water-works," "America's navy," etc.; but it is better not to imitate these expressions.[1] Such matters are matters, not of right and wrong, but of better and worse.

2. While *got* is usually better than *gotten* as a past participle, the two words have, in one case, different meanings. "I have got my lesson" is perhaps preferable to "I have gotten my lesson." But "I have got to be a scholar" means, "I must be a scholar"; while, "I have gotten to be a scholar" is, well, — perhaps a boast.

3. Good use prescribes *he drank*, but *he has drunk* [not, *he has drank*].

4. *Anybody else's*, or *anybody's else* — which is

---

[1] There are few exceptions: *day's work, week's pay*, etc.

in better use ?   For most places, the former.
Thus · " Anybody else's dog would have been
shot for his sheep-stealing."   But *anybody's else*
is often preferable at the end of the clause or
sentence.   Thus: " If the dog had been anybody
else's it would have been shot; unfortunately
it was nobody's else."   The distinction has ceased
to be a matter of logic, and become a matter of
euphony.   Of course, *else* is strictly an adjective,
and might seem to be exempt from the possessive
case.   But adjectives have always had a way of
growing fast to nouns and becoming part of them ·
e.g. sweetbriar, Redfern, Goodman.   Though *else*
is not written as a part of the noun *anybody* (which
is already long enough), it is often felt as a part
of the noun.   What you *think* is not always *anybody + else;* it is often, *anybodyelse.*   As a matter
of fact, the word *anybody* itself is really two words
grown together till we do not think of them as
adjective + noun.

Oral Exercise in Review. — Below are given a
number of sentences from Hughes's *Tom Brown's
School Days,* a book which every one likes for its
racy Saxon style, but which is not always beyond reproach in sentence-structure.   Most, however, of the sentences given below were correctly
written.   *Examine the passages, and decide as to
which of the bracketed words should be omitted.*

When several words are italicized, correct the order of them.

1. Tom's nurse was one who took in her instruction very slowly — she seemed to have two left hands and no head; and so Mrs. Brown kept her on longer than usual, that [she, the girl] might expend her awkwardness and forgetfulness upon those who would not judge and punish [her, the girl] too strictly for them.

2. It had been the immemorial habit of the village [either] to [either] christen children [either] by Bible names or [by] those of the cardinal and other virtues.

3. He was a hearty, strong boy from the first, given to fighting [with and escaping from his nurse, with his nurse and escaping from her] and fraternizing with all [of] the village boys, with whom he made expeditions all around the neighborhood.

4. You shall hear at once what sort of [a] folk the Browns are, [at least] my branch of them [at least]; and then if you don't like the sort, why cut the concern at once, and let you and [I, me] cry quits before either of us can grumble at the other.

5. For a short time after a boy has taken up [such] a life [as, like] Arnold would have urged upon him, he has a hard time of it. He finds his judgment often at fault, his body and intellect run-

ning away with him into all sorts of pitfalls, and [he, himself] coming down with a crash.

6. "No, Pompey, I must preach whenever I see a chance of being listened to, [which, and this] I never did before."

7. And now, my boys, you [who, whom] I want to get for readers, have you had enough? [Will, shall] you give in at once, and say you're convinced, and let me begin my story, or will you have more of it? Remember, I've [only] been over [only] a little bit of a hillside yet — what you could ride round easily on your ponies in an hour.

8. To-day, however, [being, being the day of] the school-house match, none of the school-house præpostors [stay, stays] by the door to watch for truants of their side; there is *carte blanche* to the school-house fags to go where they like: "They trust to our honor," as East proudly informs Tom; "they know [very well] that no school-house boy would cut the match [very well]. If he did [we'd, we should] very soon cut him, I can tell you."

9. Passing along the Ridgeway to the west for about a mile, [we come to, appears] a little clump of young beech and firs, with a growth of thorn and privet underwood.

10. I [only] know [only] two English neighborhoods thoroughly, and [in each] within a circle of five miles, [within each] there is enough of interest

and beauty to last any reasonable man his life. I believe this to be the case [almost] throughout the country [almost]; but each has a special attraction, and [neither, none] can be richer than the one I am speaking of and going to [very particularly] introduce to you [very particularly].

11. It's very odd [how, that] almost all English boys love danger.

12. He wore an old full-bottomed wig, the gift of some dandy old Brown whom he had [in the middle of the last century] valeted [in the middle of the last century], [which habiliment, a habiliment which] Master Tom looked upon with considerable respect, not to say fear.

13. [It was he, He was the one] who bent the first pin with which Tom extracted his first stickleback out of ["Pebbly Brook,"] the little stream which ran through the village, ["Pebbly Brook"]. The first stickleback was a splendid fellow, with fabulous red and blue gills. Tom kept him in a small basin till the day of [his, the fish's] death, and became a fisherman from that day.

14. His nurse told him that those good-natured looking women were in the constant habit of enticing children into the barges and taking [them, these] up to London and selling them, [which, a story which] Tom wouldn't believe.

15. "I say," said East, as soon as he [got, had gotten] his wind, looking with much increased re-

spect at Tom, "you [ain't, you're not, aren't, are not] a bad scud, not by [no, any] means."

16. But who [shall, will] tell the joy of the next morning, when the church bells were ringing a merry peal, and [in the servants' hall] old Benjy appeared [in the servants' hall] resplendent in a long blue coat and brass buttons [in the servants' hall], and a pair of old yellow buckskins and top-boots, which he had cleaned *for and inherited from Tom's grandfather.*

17. So, as we are going [to at any rate, at any rate to] see Tom Brown through his boyhood, [supposing, if] we never get any further, [which, though] (if you show a proper sense of the value of this history, there is no knowing but [that, what] we may), let us have a look at the life and environments of the child.

18. He felt [like, as if] he had been severely beaten all down his back, the natural result of his performance at his first match.

19. "And now come in and see my study; we [shall, will] have just time before dinner; and afterwards, before calling over, [we'll, we shall] do the close."

20. It [certainly] wasn't very large [certainly], being about six feet long by four broad. It couldn't be called light, as there [was, were] bars and a grating to the window; [which] little precautions [which] were necessary in the studies on the

ground floor looking out into the close, to prevent the exit of small boys [after locking up], and the entrance of contraband articles [after locking up.]

21. And now, [having broken my resolution never to write a Preface,] there are just two or three things which I [would, should] like to say a word about [having broken my resolution never to write a Preface].

22. My dear boys, old and young, you who have belonged, [or do belong,] to other schools and other houses, don't begin throwing my poor little book about the room, and abusing [me and it] [it and I], and vowing[1] you'll read no more when you get to this point. I allow you've provocation for it. But, come now, [would, should] you, any of you, give a fig for a fellow who *didn't believe in, and stand up for his own house and his own school?* You know you [wouldn't, shouldn't]. Then don't object to my cracking up the old school-house, Rugby. Haven't I a right to do it, when I'm taking all the trouble of writing this true history for all your benefits? If [you're not, you ain't] satisfied, go and write the history [of your own houses] in your own times [of your own houses] and say all you know for your own schools and houses, [provided it's true,] and [I'll, I shall] read it without abusing you [provided it's true].

[1] Is there incoherence between the clauses of this sentence after *vowing?* If so, how remedy it?

23. All the way up to London he had pondered what he [would, should] say to Tom [by way of parting advice], something that the boy could keep in his head ready for use, [by way of parting advice].

24. "I say, Green," Snooks began one night, "[ain't, isn't] that new boy, Harrison, your fag?"

"Yes; why?"

"Oh, I know something of him at home, and [would, should] like to excuse him — will you swap?"

"[Who, Whom] will you give me?"

"Well, let's see; there's Willis, Johnson — no, that won't do. Yes, I have it — there's young East, I'll give you him."

"Don't you wish you may get it?" replied Green. "I'll tell you what I'll do — I'll give you [if you like] two for Willis [if you like]."

"[Whom, Who] then?" asked Snooks.

"Hall and Brown."

"[Shouldn't, Wouldn't] have 'em at a gift."

25. By keeping out of bounds [all day], or at all events out of the house and quadrangle, [all day,] and [carefully] barring themselves [carefully] in at night, East and Tom managed to hold on without feeling very [miserably, miserable]; but it was as much as they could do.

26. His friends at home, [hadn't put him into tails] having regard, I suppose, to his age, and not

to his size and place in the school, [hadn't put him into tails]; and [even] his jackets were always too small [even]; and he had a talent for destroying clothes, and making himself look [shabbily shabby].

Oral Review-Exercise. — Correct the following sentences, after naming each fault.

1. Belonging to the modern realistic school of novelists, his address was an able defence of their tenets.

2. It is not probable that the scholars will yet give him a very lofty place, and they will be disinclined to call his books literature, but the division of sentiment as to their exact standing will not detract from the brilliancy of the future they promise.

3. "Here you are, a great, hulking fellow, endowed by providence with magnificent strength, instead of which you go about stealing nuts."

4. Cæsar and all his legions was encamped around the city, and the barbarians knew well enough it was them they had to fight, them the soldiers of the Roman god-like man.

5. "It wasn't us! it wasn't us! We wasn't there we warnt."

6. Neither of the adventurers, Olson and Lefevre, saw their native land again.

7. He sat the cage down; and the bird cried, between each mouthful, "Polly wants a cracker."

8. Like Lucretius, his pleasure was in watching the sea fight from a secure place.

9. Masquerading under the stage name of Viola Violet, there was a gasp of astonishment when she made her first entrance and was recognized by her many friends in the audience.

10. Lacking practice in what might be called the technique of acting, there was now and then some restraint in pose and gesture, and the essential element of artistic repose was lacking.

11. Passengers are warned not to get off the train while in motion.

12. Without stopping to fully describe the construction of this aural instrument, suffice it to say, that it is small and compact, and can be carried in the pocket, weighing about two ounces, constructed mostly of aluminum.

13. When I go back to Cuba again I should like to go with 10,000 interpreters instead of one, all in United States uniforms, and who would talk fast and to the point and would not expect or wait for an answer.

14. Passing a field where brother David was sowing rye, several merry voices called out, " How are you, Mr. Newton ? "

15. Mr. Adams positively declines to hang cards over the edges of the boxes at the grand opera with the names of those present in large type.

16. Eva picked up the letter from the hall table.

looked quickly round at the closed hall door, at the closed dining-room door, and at the baize door that led to the kitchen stairs — and kissed it.

17. Talking the other day with a friend (the late Mr. Keats) about Dante, he observed that whenever so great a poet told us anything in addition or continuation of an ancient story, he had a right to be regarded as classical authority.

18. Alcibiades told the Spartan envoys that if they would say to the Athenians that their power was limited and that they could only listen and then tell the Spartans what they heard that he would see that the Athenians did not join the alliance: so when the ambassadors went there they did as Alcibiades said and Alcibiades got up and said, that they could not tell two things alike and the Athenians would not have anything more to do with them and they joined the alliance.

19. Having given this department-store question much careful thought I have decided a more dangerous monopoly could not be found, for reasons as follows: First, they tend to centralize business, which is dangerous, and should not exist if we wish our city to grow and thereby equalize taxation. Second, the continuous advertising of the entire stock of an unfortunate merchant on sale in these stores at 33 cents on the dollar is not encouraging to strangers who visit us.

CHAPTER V

ON DIVIDING A PARAGRAPH INTO SENTENCES

The Sentence not its own Master. — Everybody learns at an early age some such definition as this: A sentence is the expression of a complete thought in words. But many students who have just left the grammar school are not very clear in their own minds as to what the definition means. When they come to write sentences they find it hard to decide what constitutes a complete thought. They know what the test of grammatical completeness is — the sentence must have a subject and a predicate; but they are hazy as to when the sentence is logically complete. Frankly, the most accomplished writers are sometimes troubled to decide this question. Having two ideas, they are not sure whether these ought to stand in separate sentences, or in semicolon clauses. There is no magic rule; but by the right kind of practice one may become perfectly sure, in nine cases out of ten, of the best course to take.

Perhaps the easiest way to approach the matter is to remember that the sentence is only a part of a larger unit, — the paragraph. A paragraph is either a miniature composition, or a main part of a short composition. In long works, the *chapter* is the short composition of which the paragraphs are the divisions. The sentence, in turn, is a main part of the paragraph. Whether a sentence should be long or short depends on the part it plays in the paragraph.

To make this statement plain, we need consider only the paragraph that stands alone, a miniature composition. Whatever be the number of its sentences, each forms a main part or step in the development of the paragraph-thought. All are concerned with *explaining* the same thing; each contributes something to the idea. If there is a topic sentence and this be likened to a root, the other sentences are like the stalks and leaves which grow from the root.

Note how each of the following miniature compositions[1] has a root, from which the rest of the paragraph springs necessarily.

1. *F*lowers have an expression of countenance as much as men or animals. Some seem to smile ; some have a sad expression ; some are pensive and diffident ; others again are plain, honest, and upright, like the broad-faced sunflower and the hollyhock. — H. W. BEECHER.

2. There are three wicks . . . to the lamp of a man's life ; brain, blood, and breath. Press the brain a little, its

[1] Each of these paragraphs was written as a part of a larger whole. But each is complete in itself, and may be considered as an independent whole.

light goes out, followed by both the others. Stop the heart
a minute, and out go all three of the wicks. Choke the air
out of the lungs, and presently the fluid ceases to supply the
other centres of flame, and all is soon stagnation, cold, and
darkness. — Dr. Holmes.

Consider the parts of the paragraphs just given.
Mr. Beecher has two sentences, the second group-
ing together the details which explain the first.
But the first sentence is made much shorter than
the second, because, word for word, it is to be
more emphatic. The second is the longer, because
no one of the separate clauses seemed to the writer
important enough to stand alone. The clauses of
detail taken together form one main division of the
paragraph. The short sentence that states the gist
of the paragraph is another main division. In Dr.
Holmes's brief parable, there are four sentences.
Three of them develop the general idea stated in
the first. Dr. Holmes cannot condense these three
into one explanatory sentence, as Beecher does·
he has too much to say. By giving a sentence
to each of the three " wicks," he shows that he
considers them all approximately equal in importance.

Study now another paragraph : —

It is saying less than the truth to affirm that an excellent
book (and the remark holds almost equally good of a Raph
ael as of a Milton) is like a well-chosen and well-tended
fruit tree. Its fruits are not of one season only. With the
due and natural intervals, we may recur to it year after

year, and it will supply the same nourishment and the same gratification, if only we ourselves return to it with the same healthful appetite. — COLERIDGE.

In this passage from Coleridge the first sentence is the root of the paragraph ; 'a book is like a fruit tree.' But the second sentence is made shorter than the first, because it is to state the pith of the paragraph more clearly and emphatically than did the first. The meaning of the first sentence is a little vague ; how a book is like a fruit tree, it does not say. The second sentence does say how. Note, then, that a short sentence is always emphatic, and that accordingly it should be used to state something that is important in the paragraph.

Study also the following paragraph : —

Our chief want in life, is somebody who shall make us do what we can. This is the service of a friend. With him we are easily great. There is a sublime attraction in him to whatever virtue is in us. How he flings wide the doors of existence ! What questions we ask of him ! what an understanding we have ! how few words are needed ! It is the only real society. — EMERSON.

In this paragraph of Emerson's, the main ideas are stated in brief sentences, and the summary of the paragraph comes in a sentence of six short words. But note that in the last sentence except one, the writer groups three clauses, because the three constitute parts of one main idea of the paragraph.

Read the following rather abstruse paragraphs, and decide as to which shows the chief divisions of the whole thought.

There is, first, the literature of knowledge ; and, secondly, the literature of power. The function of the first is, to teach ; the function of the second is, to move ; the first is a rudder, the second an oar or a sail. The first speaks to the mere discursive understanding ; the second speaks ultimately, it may happen, to the higher understanding or reason, but always through affections of pleasure and sympathy. — DE QUINCEY

There is, first, the literature of knowledge. And, secondly, the literature of power. The function of the first is, to teach. The function of the second is, to move. The first is a rudder. The second, an oar or a sail. The first speaks to the mere discursive understanding. The second speaks ultimately, it may happen, to the higher understanding or reason, but always through affections of pleasure and sympathy.

From a study of the foregoing selections it becomes clear that the sentence is not its own master. It is the servant of the paragraph. The paragraph, having an idea to give, uses sentences to develop this idea. A skilful writer is not in haste to crowd into a sentence all of one large, complex thought. The full expression of that thought is the task of the paragraph. The sentences are the means by which its parts may be made clear. The long sentences are for explanatory details ; the short ones are for emphatic summaries or generalizations, and for rapid narrative.

Sentence Unity.—I. *A sentence that possesses Unity of Substance constitutes one main step in the development of the paragraph-idea.* A main step, as thus employed, usually means a sentence giving one of the following: (1) the general subject of the paragraph; (2) the general thought or assertion of the paragraph; (3) the repetition of a preceding idea in new words; (4) an illustration; (5) a group of particulars or details; (6) one proof, or term, in a chain of reasoning; (7) a brief contrast; (8) a cause and an effect; (9) an assertion and a very brief illustration. It would be absurd to hold these principles of unity anxiously in mind when one is writing. Having thought them over a little, and taken to heart the general doctrine that the sentence should be one main step, the scholar should trust his own sense of unity. The chief value of any such analysis is that it may help the scholar to give thought to his own sentences.

II. *A sentence that possesses Unity of Form keeps one coherent structure throughout, and subordinates unimportant clauses to the important.* Unity of form does not concern the division of the paragraph into sentences. It will be considered in Chapter VI., under Well-knit Sentences.

I. Unity of Substance by Excluding Irrelevant Ideas.—Perhaps the first thing that is noticed in reading hasty composition, is that some sentences are too long. Here is one, written by a lad of fourteen. It will seem to most readers to be a sentence of infantine simplicity, such as no high school student is in the slightest danger of perpetrating. My apology for giving it is that it renders every heterogeneous sentence ridiculous.

Oliver Orlando's brother did not like him and when he heard that Orlando whipped Charles he was very angry and was going to burn Orlando's house up with him in it, but Adam, Orlando's faithful servant, ran out and told him, so they got all the money they had and started for the forest of Arden, when they got pretty near there Adam being so old fainted from hunger.

The student who wrote this was not thinking of the parts of his paragraph; he was thinking merely of the story of *As You Like It*. He plunged ahead after the story, never looking behind him. The result is a long, rambling sentence, with several chief thoughts in it. These chief thoughts are four: (1) Oliver hatefully plots to kill Orlando. (2) Adam foils Oliver. (3) Adam and Orlando flee. (4) Adam at last faints. The paragraph therefore divides into four decent, though childish, sentences : —

Oliver, Orlando's brother, did not like him ; and when he heard that Orlando whipped Charles he was very angry, and was going to burn Orlando's house up with him in it. But Adam, Orlando's faithful servant, ran out and told him. So they got together all the money they had, and started for the forest of Arden. When they got pretty near there, Adam, being so old, fainted from hunger.

Periods are now substituted for several of the student's commas. That writer had confused these two marks, the comma and the full stop. Such an error may be called, for mere convenience, *the comma fault.* It is readily seen that of all possible mistakes in punctuation, the comma fault is the most serious and elementary. To begin a new sentence after a comma is an infallible sign of illiteracy.

Oral Exercise. — In the following passages, correct the comma fault wherever it appears. Change the sentences in other ways to give a more mature tone to them.

1. I don't know what to do in such a case, it is too hard to decide. [Change comma to semicolon.]

2. Romeo fell in love at once, he couldn't help himself, he had never seen any person so lovable.

3. So they also started for the forest of Arden disguised as a countryman and woman, when they got there they bought a house that was to be sold at auction, once while wandering around they met Orlando and Rosalind asked him if it was he that was spoiling the trees by carving love sentences on them, and he said it was, so she said he could pretend that she was Rosalind, so he came there every day until one day he was detained by seeing a lioness just going to spring on Oliver.

Theme. — Write a paragraph of six to ten short sentences. Let the first state the whole event in brief.   Let the others give the steps of the action tersely, rapidly, emphatically.   Revise for spelling and punctuation.   Suggested topics : —

1.   Shooting the rapids.
2.   How the water comes down at the falls.
3.   How the accident happened.
4.   How a log-jam is broken.
5.   The way to shoot a glass ball.
6.   Down a hill on a wheel.
7.   Sights from a car window.
8.   A fall on the ice.
9.   Shooting the "Chutes."
10.   A runaway.
11.   A flash-light photograph.
12.   How the bird (or game) escaped.
13.   Paul Revere's ride.
14.   An exciting moment.

II.   Unity of Substance by Including all the Parts of an Idea. — It has already been said that a paragraph may be composed of several very short sentences, each one a main step of the paragraph, each one a unit.   For example : —

A great silence made itself felt.   Then, on a sudden, a dry sound cracked in the air.   The viscount had slapped his adversary's face.   Every one rose to interfere.   Cards were exchanged between the two.

Here, indeed, it may be that the second and third sentences are halves of one idea, divided to make its parts more emphatic. At all events, while a sentence may be very short and still constitute a principal factor of the paragraph, sentences should not be so brief that each is, so to speak, only half a main thought. A main thought may be composite. Thus, it is often effective (*a*) to *state* and to *explain* an idea very briefly, within the one sentence; (*b*) to show an extremely close relation of *cause* and *effect*, by stating both within the one sentence; (*c*) to *contrast* two things very briefly within the one sentence.

Now, a child gives his ideas in mere bits; he cannot express the relations of the bits to each other. For example: —

My aunt was a very large woman. My uncle was a very thin man. He was very delicate. He dwindled. I mean, he got thinner and punier every day. And my aunt thought a great deal of him. She wished him to get well. She gave him a great deal of medicine. She gave him so much that he began to get worse. He finally died.

This paragraph tells the story of how a woman doctored her husband to death. The writer has made eight steps in the story, which perhaps has not really more than four main parts: (1) The *contrast* between my aunt and uncle. (2) My uncle " dwindled " — *explained* by saying he got punier daily. (3) My aunt's love, and its *consequence* — her wish for my uncle's recovery. (4) The form the wish took, — giving of medicine. (5) The twofold result, — aggravation of the disease, then death.

The original sentences may be combined into four. In combining them, what pointing shall be used instead of so many full stops ? We may use commas, but only if we make one clause dependent or join two clauses or propositions by a conjunction. We may say, for example, " My aunt was a very large woman, and my uncle a very thin, delicate man." We have inserted an *and;* this permits the use of a comma. The result is a pretty good sentence, having one complex idea, — the contrast between the ample lady and her slight husband.

But another invaluable means of showing the real *factors* of the sentence is the semicolon. The semicolon, as was said in Chapter III., is a kind of weak full stop. Nearly always it connects statements that are unrelated and independent grammatically, but intimately related in sense. In a way,[1] the semicolon connects sentences, a period separates sentences. The former sign is priceless to the writer who, when he comes to expand each idea of his paragraph, finds the structure growing too complicated. He has merely to place a semicolon and go ahead with a miniature new sentence, which every reader will understand to be a part of the logical unit in hand.

[1] In another and larger sense, every mark of punctuation is disjunctive, as was said on page 21.

If we combine the eight sentences by the help of the semicolon, we get four, somewhat like the following : —

My aunt was a very large woman ; my uncle, on the contrary, was a very thin delicate man. He dwindled ; that is, he got thinner and punier every day. My aunt thought a good deal of him, and naturally she wished him to get well. She gave him, accordingly, a great deal of medicine. She gave him so much indeed that he began to get worse ; and, finally, he died.

Most students do not use the semicolon enough. Two or three semicolon clauses, however, are sufficient for a very long sentence. If more are written there is usually danger of encroaching upon the next main thought of the paragraph. *It is better to write too many short sentences than too many long ones.*

Oral Exercise. — Consider the following paragraph, and decide whether the main thoughts of it are nine, as here indicated, or four. If four, the thoughts are : (1) Contrast between light above and dark below. (2) The growing dark. (3) The faint, weird sights and sounds that come to the narrator. (4) His retreat from the abbey. If, having given the matter careful thought, you think there should be but four sentences, or if you think there is any other fault in the punctuation, explain how you would repoint.

The last beams of day were now faintly streaming through the painted windows in the high vaults above me. The lower parts of the abbey were already wrapped in the obscurity of twilight. The chapels and aisles grew darker and darker. The effigies of the kings faded into shadows. The marble figures of the monuments assumed strange shapes in the uncertain light. The evening breeze crept through the aisles like the cold breath of the grave. And even the distant footfall of a verger, traversing the Poet's Corner, had something strange and dreary in its sound. I slowly retraced my morning's walk. And as I passed out at the portal of the cloisters, the door, closing with a jarring noise behind me, filled the whole building with echoes.

Punctuation for Emphasis. — Below are given three ways of punctuating the same words. We may suppose the same words to be used by three different generals.

1. General A. twirled his moustache, and spoke softly, in his calm, unruffled way, as if he were explaining a mathematical problem to a cadet; he said to the soldier, " You are a coward : you shrink, you dodge, you hide, you run away when the danger comes." He spoke meditatively, and with a little drawl, letting his voice rise at each pause.

2. General B. looked at the soldier steadily, and said in a sharp, decided tone : " You are a coward: you shrink ; you dodge ; you hide ; you run away when the danger comes.

3. General C. sprang up from his camp-stool, angry and indignant. He spoke explosively and incoherently. " You are a coward ! You shrink.

You dodge. You hide. You run away when the danger comes."

Evidently the punctuation here is largely dependent on the different states of mind. A calm, logical attitude is reflected in the nice distinctions conveyed by the colon and comma. An excited mood over-emphasizes each detail, and makes it a sentence. There is sometimes need of indignant emphasis on each detail. Perhaps therefore the strict unity of the sentence may sometimes be sacrificed for the sake of emphasis. Such a sacrifice however should very rarely be made.

Oral Exercise. — Consider the following paragraph as a whole, and decide whether the sentences represent the main factors of the paragraph-thought. If you agree that "the song of a young girl's voice" is as important in the paragraph as several of the other songs put together, how can this importance be indicated by punctuation?

The first thing which Tom saw was the black cedars, high and sharp against the rosy dawn. And St. Brandan's Isle reflected double in the still broad silver sea. The wind sung softly in the cedars, and the water sung among the caves. The sea-birds sung as they streamed out into the ocean, and the land-birds as they built among the boughs. And the air was so full of song that it stirred St. Brandan and his hermits, as they slumbered in the shade. And they moved their good old lips, and sung their good old hymn amid their dreams. But among all the songs one came across the water more sweet and clear than all, for it was the song of a young girl's voice.

Theme. — Write a paragraph of four sentences on one of the following subjects. Let the first sentence be a general statement. Then let each of three compound sentences group together details, and so explain the first.

1. The three parts of a tree, and their characteristics.

2. The three parts of my town.

3. A picture I like : its background, its figures, its coloring.

4. The lunch-room.

5. A sleeping-car: the car itself, the travellers, the porter.

6. Uses of a jack-knife: legitimate, illegitimate, doubtful.

7. Three men representing three kinds of true Americanism.

8. Three great men, typically English.

9. Three great men typically Roman.

10. Three types of philanthropist.

11. Three kinds of coward.

12. Three kinds of hero.

13. Three noble American women.

14. Three women who write stories.

Written Exercise. — In the seventeenth century there were many authors whose minds were full of Latin models. These writers tried to build up in English, an uninflected language, sentences as complex as those of Cicero. They tried to make the sentence do the work of the paragraph. How utterly they failed may be seen in the following passages from Defoe and Lord Clarendon. Considering each selection as a paragraph, rewrite with reference to unity of substance in the sentence.

1. There is one thing more remarkable in this parish, and it is this : twenty-six sheets of lead, hanging all together, were blown off from the middle isle of our church, and were carried over the north isle, which is a very large one, without touching it ; and into the churchyard ten yards' distance from the church ; and they were took up all joined together as they were on the roof ; the plumber told me that the sheets weighed each three hundred and a half, one with another. This is what is most observable in our parish : but I shall give you an account of one thing (which perhaps you may have from other hands) that happened in another, called Kingscote, a little village about three miles from Tedbury, and seven from us : where William Kingscote, Esq., has many woods ; among which was one grove of very tall trees, being each near eighty foot high ; the which he greatly valued for the tallness and prospect of them, and therefore resolved never to cut them down : but it so happened, that six hundred of them, within the compass of five acres were wholly blown down ; (and supposed to be much at the same time) each tree tearing up the ground with its root ; so that the roots of most of the trees, with the turf and earth about them, stood up at least fifteen or sixteen foot high; the lying down of which trees is an amazing sight to all beholders. — *Defoe.*

2. It is true, that as he[1] was of a most incomparable gentleness, application, and even submission to good and worthy and entire men, so he was naturally (which could not be

[1] That is, Lord Falkland.

more evident in his place, which objected him to another conversation and intermixture than his own election would have done) *adversus malos injucundus ;* and was so ill a dissembler of his dislike and disinclination to ill men, that it was not possible for such not to discern it.   There was once, in the House of Commons, such a declared acceptation of the good service an eminent member had done to them, and, as they said, to the whole kingdom, that it was moved, he being present, "That the speaker might, in the name of the whole house, give him thanks, and then that every member might, as a testimony of his particular acknowledgment, stir or move his hat towards him ; the which (though not ordered) when very many did, the lord Falkland (who believed the service itself not to be of that moment, and that an honourable and generous person could not have stooped to it for any recompence) instead of moving his hat, stretched both his arms out, and clasped his hands together upon the crown of his hat, and held it close down to his head ; that all men might see, how odious that flattery was to him, and that very approbation of the person, though at the same time most popular. — *Clarendon.*

Oral Exercise. — Examine the paragraphs by Hawthorne (p. 106), Macaulay, Webster, Huxley (pp. 107–8) to see whether the sentences are units in substance.   Note also the different effects produced by long and short sentences.

III. A.   Unity of Substance by Keeping to the Point. — In a hastily written manuscript will often be found unlike ideas joined together in one sentence.   Some persons are worse than others in this matter, but everybody, in composing rapidly, is liable to the fault.   It is amusingly easy to fly off at a tangent, if the parts of the paragraph have not been properly thought out. The mind often works erratically; it is pursuing a given idea when some word used suggests a different line of thinking and the train is switched off its track.

Cardinal Newman once wrote a burlesque of this scatter-brained kind of writing. He pretends that the lad is writing a theme on the topic, " Fortune favors the brave." In the midst of it the boy says : —

Napoleon, too, shows us how little we can rely on fortune ; but his faults, great as they were, are being redeemed by his nephew, Louis Napoleon, who has shown himself very different from what was expected, though he has never explained how he came to swear to the constitution, and then mounted the imperial throne.

Here the writer has not committed the comma fault; he has not begun an independent sentence after a comma. But he has set down ideas irrelevant to the sentence, and, in this case, irrelevant even to the theme.

This lack of unity often arises from putting down, as the sentence proceeds, the details that occur parenthetically to the writer; he empties his mind upon the paper. Thus : —

My aunt happened to notice, as she stood looking into the glass and thinking how pretty she was, for she was really pretty for one so old, that the eyes of a portrait or one of the eyes was moving, for my aunt had a large picture of my uncle in her room in her country-house, which was in Derbyshire.

B. Many a sentence which ends in an irrelevant clause can be made to show unity by the insertion of some intermediate link that occurred in the mind but was overlooked in the writing. "Johnson wrote political articles, and took care that the Whigs did not get the best of it," becomes a unit if we supply a few words : "Johnson wrote political articles, *and in those which referred to parliamentary debates* took care that the Whigs did not get the best of it." In other words, a sentence must not merely include the *expressed* parts of a main thought, as in the second kind of unity of substance; it must *express* every part of the main thought.

Oral Exercise. — Trim the following sentences into shape, so that each shall be a unit. If necessary, divide the sentence.

1. He was young; but his foolishness stood him in good stead.

2. The cholera in Egypt is assuming a more loathsome form, among the dead being Major Roddy Owen, the famous Uganda explorer.

3. The delegates, wearied by the excitement of the past week, have hurried to their homes, a few remaining for all the business men have been making unusual displays in spite of the hard times.

4. The new light is placed upon a gas-jet, which supplies the gas to a curious film, which is made of

some chemically prepared substance that becomes incandescent, not having to be changed oftener than twice a year, if you are careful with it.

5. The electric lights, which are of the Edison pattern, are not burned later than six o'clock. They are more convenient than gas, and they come packed in straw.

Oral Exercise, in Review. — Decide whether the following sentences are units or not. Indicate which form of sentence unity each has or lacks. Suggest improvements.

1. In the midst of life we are in death, and it has been said that the tariff is a tax.

2. Jesu! Jesu! Dead! — he drew a good bow; — and dead! — he shot a fine shoot: — John of Gaunt loved him well, and betted much money on his head. — *2 Henry IV.*, Act III., Sc. 2, l. 48.

3. He had one claw knobbed and the other jagged; and Tom delighted in watching him hold on to the sea-weed with his knobbed claw, while he cut up salads with his jagged one, and then put them into his mouth, after smelling at them, like a monkey, and always the little barnacles threw out their casting nets and swept the water, and came in for their share of whatever there was for dinner.

4. We were now thoroughly broken down, but the intense excitement of the time denied us repose, and after a unique slumber of some three or four

hours' duration, we arose, as if by preconcert, to make examination of our treasure.

5. Thou didst swear to me upon a parcel-gilt [partly-gilt] goblet, sitting in my Dolphin-chamber, at the round table, by a sea-coal fire, upon Wednesday in Whitsun week, when the prince broke thy head for likening his father to a singing man of Windsor; thou didst swear to me then, as I was washing thy wound, to marry me, and make me my lady thy wife. — *2 Henry IV.*, Act II., Sc. 1, l. 94.

6. There was something in the tone of this note which gave me great uneasiness. Its whole style differed materially from that of Legrand; what could he be dreaming of? what new crotchet possessed his excitable brain? what "business of the highest importance" could *he* possibly have to transact? Jupiter's account of him boded no good; I dreaded lest the continued pressure of misfortune had, at length, fairly unsettled the reason of my friend; without a moment's hesitation, therefore, I prepared to accompany the negro.

7. And in that country is an old castle, that stands upon a rock, the which is cleped the Castle of the sparrowhawk, that is beyond the city of Layas, beside the town of Parsipee, that belongeth to the lordship of Cruk; that[1] is a rich lord and a good Christian man; where men find a sparrow-

---

[1] This " that " is demonstrative.

hawk upon a perch right fair and right well made; and a fair Lady of Fayryre, that keepeth it. — *Mandeville.*

8. And thus will the city have more lights on the subject, and what will be a gain in lighting to the city will be a greater loss in cash, and the city's loss will be the Water Works company's gain, and we are glad of it so far as the company is concerned for the company was put off and were refused a renewal of its contract with the city at terms that were most reasonable, and the company will also make up for lost time now in good shape.

CHAPTER VI

ON WELL-KNIT SENTENCES

A sentence may be said to be well-knit if it stands the following tests. It must have unity of form; freedom from excessive looseness; a due amount of emphasis; and climax, if climax is required. All these technical terms need explanation.

Unity of Form. — To be a unit of form, a sentence must place subordinate thoughts in subordinate clauses, and must keep one coherent structure throughout.

Subordination of Clauses. — In the early years of a language, before it has been used to express philosophy and science, the structure of the sentences is loose and simple; it sounds like the speech of a child. Here is a passage from a book which appeared about 1370, as the *Voyage and Travels of Sir John Mandeville*. There is some doubt whether or not there was really a Sir John; but these Travels are very interesting and curious reading.

And some men say that in the Isle of Lango is yet the daughter of Hippocrates, in form and likeness of a great dragon, that is a hundred fathom of length, as men say: for I have not seen her. And they of the Isles call her, Lady of the Land. And she lieth in an old castle, in a cave, and sheweth twice or thrice in the year. And she doth no harm to no man, but if men do her harm. And she was thus changed and transformed, from a fair damsel, into likeness of a dragon, by a goddess, that was cleped Diana. And men say, that she shall so endure in that form of a dragon, unto the time that a knight come, that is so hardy, that dare come to her and kiss her on the mouth: and then shall she turn again to her own kind, and be a woman again. But after that she shall not live long.

Though much of the naïve, childlike quality of this passage is due to the archaic phraseology, much also is due to the use of *and* and *but* instead of other conjunctions.

In certain kinds of writing it is natural enough that ideas should be strung together with *and*'s. Thus: "It rained, and hailed, and blew, and snowed, and froze, and they became weary of winter." But suppose that they did not weary of winter. The sentence then would run, "Though it rained, and hailed, and snowed, and froze, they did not become weary of winter." Here we have ceased the mere enumeration of things that happened, one after the other, and have stated a process of reasoning. The result is a complex sentence. The ability to construct good complex sentences means ability to do careful thinking.

H

In every complex sentence there is some one *proposition* that ought to stand out, with the high light upon it. This is the thing we most wish to say; to change the comparison, it is the heart of the sentence. If the other parts can be made subordinate to it, the strongest kind of sentence unity is secured. In the sentence, "It rained; it snowed; it hailed; they did not weary of winter," all the assertions are stated as equally important. But, clearly enough, the last one is the kernel of the sentence. Therefore the preceding clauses ought to be reduced to their proper rank by being made dependent.

Oral Exercise. — Examine the following compound sentences, to decide whether or not there is in each some important thought to which the others ought to have been subordinated. Then improve the unity by reducing the subordinate ideas to dependent clauses having a participle. or a relative adverb like *when*.

1. Love is blind; it is not for want of eyes.
2. The soldiers were perhaps somewhat sleepy with the sultriness of the afternoon; they had now laid by much of their vigilance.
3. I spied an honest fellow coming along a lane, and asked him if he had ever heard of a house called the house of Shaws.
4. The next person I came across was a dapper

little man in a beautiful white wig; I knew well that barbers were great gossips, and I asked him plainly what kind of a man was Mr. Balfour of the Shaws.

5. In these days folk still believed in witches and trembled at a curse; and this curse fell pat, like a wayside omen, to arrest me; it took the pith out of my legs.

6. I was called in at last; my uncle counted out into my hand seven and thirty golden guinea pieces.

7. I had come close to one of the turns in the stair; I felt my way as usual; my hand slipped upon an edge and found nothing but emptiness beyond it.

8. I returned to the kitchen; I made up such a blaze as had not shone there for many a long year; I wrapped myself in my plaid; I lay down upon the chests and fell asleep.

The So Construction. — The conjunction *so* is a useful word, and the learner prefers it to its synonyms, *therefore* and *consequently*, because it is simpler, less formal than either. But in a narrative which is liberally besprinkled with *so*'s the reader feels that the simplicity is overdone. Here is an extreme example.

A short time afterward my uncle died; so my aunt went to her country-house in Derbyshire. She did not wish to be alone in the country; so she took her servants. When they got there they found the house very lonely; so the maids did not want to stay, but they did.

Examine the sentences just quoted, and show the relations between the clauses by other devices than the use of *so*.

So, as a conjunction, should be employed very sparingly. When it is employed, it should usually be preceded by *a semicolon rather than a comma*.

Oral Exercise. — A careful writer is known by his use of conjunctions: he does not use *and* unless the clauses joined are co-ordinate; nor *but* unless there is a real opposition; nor a given subordinate conjunction unless it is actually required by logic. In the subjoined selections from Ruskin the original conjunctions have been changed to those in italics. Find better expressions for those italicized.

1. In employing all the muscular power at our disposal we are to make the employments we choose as educational as possible. *Consequently* a wholesome human employment is the first and best method of education, mental as well as bodily. A man taught to plough, row, or steer well, *moreover* a woman taught to cook properly, and make a dress neatly, are already educated in many essential moral habits. Labour considered as a discipline has hitherto been thought of only for criminals, *therefore* the real and noblest function of labour is to prevent crime, *but* not to be Re-formatory, but Formatory. — RUSKIN.

2. We must spend our money in some way, at some time, *accordingly* it cannot at any time be spent without employing somebody. *Vhile* we gamble it away, the person who wins it must spend it; *while* we lose it in a railroad speen-lation, it has gone into some one else's pockets, or merely gone to pay navvies for making a useless embankment, *but*

not to pay riband or button makers for making useless ribands or buttons; we cannot lose it (unless by actually destroying it) *and not give* employment of some kind; *nevertheless* whatever quantity of money exists, the relative quantity of employment must some day come out of it; *and* the distress of the nation signifies that the employments given have produced nothing that will support its existence. Men cannot live on ribands, or buttons, or velvet, or by going quickly from place to place; *but* every coin spent in useless ornament, or useless motion, is so much withdrawn from the national means of life. — RUSKIN.

One Coherent Structure. — We have seen that to be well-knit a sentence must have that unity of form which gives every thought its proper clause-rank. It must also be uniform in structure. There should be no sudden, unnecessary change in subject, or in the form of the verb. Sometimes a sentence is pulled about by the mind as a child by a cross nurse. It begins in the active voice, it is twitched aside into the passive. It begins as the act of one person, it ends as that of another. Even so admirable a writer as John Fiske has this sentence · "But Howe could not bear to acknowledge the defeat of his attempts to storm, and accordingly, at five o'clock, with genuine British persistency, a third attack was ordered." This "British persistency" is evidently Howe's. Why not give him full credit for it, thus? — "But Howe could not bear to acknowledge the defeat of his attempts to storm, and accordingly, at five o'clock, with genuine British persistency he ordered a third attack."

Oral Exercise. — Change the following sentences so that each shall have unity of form.

1. A blue pencil? there is nothing so easy for an editor to manage, so unmistakable in reading, so wholly impressive to a contributor when he sees it.

2. Tom and East became good friends, and the tyranny of a certain insolent fellow was sturdily resisted by them together.

3. You will see no sudden jerks of the *St. Ambrose* rudder, nor will any clumsy rounding of a point be seen.

4. Miller, motionless till now, lifts his right hand and the tassel is whirled round his head.

5. Thorold had just read the account of John Inglesant's vision of the dead King Charles. He disliked the idea of spending the night in the old country house, and still more to go through the tapestried chamber; but it was immediately determined by him that such an invitation must not be refused.

The Loose Sentence. — The passage given at the beginning of the chapter, from Mandeville, is written in what are called loose sentences. *Loose* as applied to a sentence, does not necessarily mean that the sentence is bad, — that it is rambling or disjointed. A loose sentence is one in which an independent statement comes first, followed by others, dependent or independent. Example:

"And some men say that in the Isle of Lango is yet the daughter of Hippocrates, in form and likeness of a great dragon, that is a hundred fathom of length, as men say: for I have not seen her." In this sentence comes first a proposition, — "And some men say," followed by several subordinate clauses, and by one independent clause, — "for I have not seen her." The test of a loose sentence is a grammatical one: the sentence can be closed at some point before the end, without hurting the grammatical structure. At what places in the sentence just quoted is the grammatical structure complete?

The loose sentence is used freely in conversation. The speaker gives his main idea first, and qualifies it afterward. Therefore the legitimate effect of the loose sentence is to lend an air of simplicity, a colloquial air, to the style. The danger is that it may become a mere sequence of clauses, that dangle insecurely, each from the preceding, like needles hanging from a magnet. Avoid long loose sentences.

Examine the sentence by Defoe, p. 89. It is a fine example of what a loose sentence should not be.

The Periodic Sentence. — In the sentence, " A short time afterward my uncle died; so my aunt went to her country-house in Derbyshire," the grammatical structure is complete at "died." But

if the two clauses be welded together by *because,*
they will no longer be grammatically free.   Thus:
"Because my uncle died shortly afterward, my aunt
went to her country-house in Derbyshire."   This
sentence is periodic in form.   A periodic sentence
is a complex sentence in which the modifiers of
the verb precede the verb.   The effect of this
structure is to delay the main idea of the sentence until the last.[1]   Obviously, if too many
subordinate ideas occur before the main one, the
mind of the reader will weary with the tension
of expectation.   Short periodic sentences however
are extremely effective in arousing the reader's
attention and holding it till the important idea
is stated.   It is plain that good periodic structure
is highly conducive to unity in the sentence: each
subordinate idea is held in its proper place of subordination till the main idea is stated, and on the
reader is flashed a pleasant sense that the structure
has grown naturally into one complete whole.

Oral Exercise — Examine the oral exercise on
pages 98, 99, and say which sentences were made
periodic in the effort to improve their unity.

[1] Sometimes a simple sentence is called periodic. This is
when the natural order of subject and predicate is inverted.
Thus: " Great is Diana of the Ephesians." Indeed, the attribu-
tive position of the adjective is sometimes called periodic, because it delays the noun-idea. A long sentence is sometimes
periodic up to a certain point, then loose; sometimes the opposite is true.

Oral Exercise. — Below are given some good peri-odic sentences.[1] Give equivalent loose sentences. Decide whether or not the loose are better than the periodic.

1. At this moment a large, comfortable white house, that had been heretofore hidden by green trees, came into view.

[Changed, this might read : " A large, comfortable white house had been heretofore hidden by green trees; it came into view at this moment."]

2. Off went Timothy's hat.

3. And it was to this household that Timothy had brought his child for adoption.

4. Gay, not being used to a regular morning toilet, had fought against it valiantly at first.

5. If you care to feel a warm glow in the region of your heart, imagine little Timothy Jessup sent to play in that garden.

6. Yet of an evening, or on Sunday, she was no village gossip.

Oral Exercise. — The following passage, from Hawthorne, is written in excellent loose sentences. Change to periodic all of them that can be so changed without hurting the ease of structure. Whatever else it be, a periodic sentence should never be strained or unnatural.

[1] Sentences that are in the main periodic may ordinarily be given this name.

Then Theseus bent himself in good earnest to the task, and strained every sinew with manly strength and resolution. He put his whole brave heart into the effort. He wrestled with the big and sluggish stone as if it had been a living enemy. He heaved, he lifted, he resolved now to succeed, or else to perish there, and let the rock be his monument forever! Æthra stood gazing at him, and clasped her hands, partly with a mother's pride, and partly with a mother's sorrow. The great rock stirred! Yes, it was raised slowly from the bedded moss and earth, uprooting the shrubs and flowers along with it, and was turned upon its side. Theseus had conquered!

Inappropriate Periodicity. — It is foolish to use an elaborate suspended structure when a very simple thought or a very rapid narrative is to be given. Note the pomposity of the following sentences. Remove it by changing the structure.

"Three summers ago, to rejoin my family in northern Michigan, I left the city. On a little peninsula which juts out into Lake Michigan, a group of houses, dignified by the name of Edgewood, stands. Undistracted by the bustle of hotel life, a few sensible people live here. To get away from town for a few days and lounge in the pine woods about Edgewood, to me is always very pleasant."

Oral Exercise. — Examine the following sentences one by one, and say whether each is (*a*) wholly periodic, (*b*) wholly loose, or (*c*) partly loose and partly periodic. When the last is the case, show at what point the change of structure occurs.

1. He who walks in the way these following ballads point will be manful in necessary fight, fair in trade, loyal in love, generous to the poor, tender in the household, prudent in living, plain in speech, merry upon occasion, simple in behavior, and honest in all things. — LANIER.

2. While Johnson was busied with his *Idlers*, his mother, who had accomplished her ninetieth year, died at Lichfield. It was long since he had seen her; but he had not failed to contribute largely, out of his small means, to her comfort. In order to defray the charges of her funeral, and to pay some debts which she had left, he wrote a little book in a single week, and sent off the sheets to the press without reading them over. A hundred pounds were paid him for the copyright; and the purchasers had great cause to be pleased with their bargain, for the book was "Rasselas." MACAULAY : *Life of Johnson.*

3. Finally, brethren, whatsoever things are true, whatsoever things are honest, whatsoever things are just, whatsoever things are pure, whatsoever things are lovely, whatsoever things are of good report; if there be any virtue, and if there be any praise, think on these things. — *Philippians.*

4. "Sir, you may destroy this little institution; it is weak; it is in your hands! I know it is one of the lesser lights in the literary horizon of our country. You may put it out. But, if you do so, you must carry through your work! You must extinguish, one after another, all those greater lights of science which, for more than a century, have thrown their radiance over our land! It is, Sir, as I have said, a small college. And yet there are those who love it." WEBSTER.

5. Sir, let me recur to pleasing recollections; let me indulge in refreshing remembrance of the past; let me remind you that, in early times, no States cherished greater harmony, both of principle and feeling, than Massachusetts and South Carolina. Would to God that harmony might again return! Shoulder to shoulder they went through the

Revolution; hand in hand they stood round the administration of Washington, and felt his own great arm lean on them for support. Unkind feeling, if it exist, alienation and distrust, are the growth, unnatural to such soils, of false principles since sown. They are weeds, the seeds of which that same great arm never scattered. — WEBSTER.

6. That man, I think, has had a liberal education, who has been so trained in youth that his body is the ready servant of his will, and does with ease and pleasure all the work that, as a mechanism, it is capable of; whose intellect is a clear, cold, logic engine, with all its parts of equal strength, and in smooth working order; ready, like a steam engine, to be turned to any kind of work, and spin the gossamers as well as forge the anchors of the mind; whose mind is stored with a knowledge of the great and fundamental truths of Nature and of the laws of her operations; one who, no stunted ascetic, is full of life and fire, but whose passions are trained to come to heel by a vigorous will, the servant of a tender conscience; who has learned to love all beauty, whether of Nature or of art, to hate all vileness, and to respect others as himself. — HUXLEY.

7. If then the power of speech is a gift as great as any that can be named, — if the origin of language is by many philosophers even considered to be nothing short of divine, — if by means of words the secrets of the heart are brought to light, pain of soul is relieved, hidden grief is carried off, sympathy conveyed, counsel imparted, experience recorded, and wisdom perpetuated, — if by great authors the many are drawn up into unity, national character is fixed, a people speaks, the past and the future, the East and the West are brought into communication with each other, — if such men are, in a word, the spokesmen and prophets of the human family, — it will not answer to make light of Literature or to neglect its study; rather we may be sure that, in proportion as we master it in whatever language, and imbibe its spirit, we shall ourselves become in our own measure the ministers of like benefits to others, be they

many or few, be they in the obscurer or the more distinguished walks of life, — who are united to us by social ties, and are within the sphere of our personal influence. — CARDINAL NEWMAN.[1]

Oral Exercise. — Each of the passages given above should be read aloud as a whole, to get the effects produced by the different types of sentence. In the first passage note that the first clause arouses interest by the periodic structure. So do the first and third sentences in the second passage; but the third and fourth — loose — have a fine simplicity that adds to the weight of their subject matter. The third passage moves up steadily to an impressive point, — the word *think*. The fourth passage is extremely direct and earnest. Webster is pleading for his *Alma Mater*, Dartmouth; is making an appeal, straight from his heart. Almost choked with emotion, he has no desire to frame periodic sentences and nicely subordinated clauses. In the fifth passage he is perhaps equally direct; but he is master of himself, and his sentences are somewhat more elaborate. In the sixth passage, Huxley gets a steadily increasing strength of thought, but not of structure. Cardinal Newman, on the other hand, builds up his period with superb suspense both of form and thought.

Written Exercise. — Change the sentence by Huxley into the periodic form. This can be done by

[1] The longer passages to which the last two selections belong may be found in Genung's *Rhetorical Analysis*.

changing the order of clauses, and beginning each subordinate clause with *if*, or with *suppose*, or with a relative.

Emphasis in the Sentence. — A sentence cannot be called well-knit if it does not succeed in calling most attention to the most important idea. We have seen already how important it is to put the unimportant parts of the sentence into subordinate clauses. How may further emphasis be had?

The beginning and the end of the sentence are the most prominent places. Important words should usually stand in these places. Rarely should these points be covered up with trivial expressions. Compare two sentences. "As a matter of fact, it is bread, rather than advice, that people actually need, in this city." "Bread it is, rather than advice, that, in this city, people actually need."

Attention can always be called to a word by placing it out of the ordinary, commonplace order. The *inverted* order, where verb precedes the noun, or predicate adjective precedes the verb, frequently permits emphasis to be put just where it is wanted. The oft-quoted example is as good a one as can be found· "Great is Diana of the Ephesians!" How much better it is, how much *greater* the cry is than, "Diana of the Ephesians is great!"

Oral Exercise. —Which of the following sentences from Ruskin begin and end with words that deserve distinction?[1]

" For all books are divisible into two classes, — the books of the hour, and the books of all time. Mark this distinction; it is not one of quality only. It is not merely the bad book that does not last, and the good one that does; it is a distinction of species. There are good books for the hour, and good ones for all time; bad books for the hour, and bad ones for all time. I must define the two kinds before I go farther."

Oral Exercise. — Change the order of words in the following sentences so as to throw more emphasis on the italicized words. Avoid infringement of English idiom in making the changes.

1. It is *courage* that wins.

2. Never say *die,* under any circumstances.

3. Yet he stood *beautiful and bright,* as born to rule the storm.

4. A rascal, *nothing more or less,* he was.

5. Gilpin went *away,* and the post boy went *away.*

6. The English child is *white as an angel.*

7. When wild northwesters rave *on stormy nights* With wind and wave *how proud a thing* to fight.

[1] The phrase, "words that deserve distinction," is Professor Barrett Wendell's. See his *English Composition,* p. 103 (Scribner's).

8. What a piece of work *man* is!

9. Trafalgar lay, full in face, *bluish* mid the burning water.

10. He repeatedly pronounced *these words,* and they were the last which he uttered.

11. The king said, "*Alas,* help me from hence."

12. Man is *the paragon of animals,* the beauty of the world.

13. What a place an old *library* is to be in. It seems as though all the souls of all the writers that have bequeathed their labors to these Bodleians, as in some *middle state* or dormitory, were reposing here. I do not want to handle, to profane their *winding sheet,* the leaves. I could a *shade* as soon dislodge.

Climax. — The principle of climax demands that in a series of related terms the weaker degree should precede the stronger. Southey says of Lord Nelson's being permitted to live to hear the news of his great victory: "That consolation, that joy, that triumph, was afforded him." By these three nouns the reader ascends, as if by a ladder — climax is merely Greek for ladder. Endeavor to discover the original order in which the following sentences were written to secure climax. Changing them by slight omissions, weave them together into two sentences.

"The most triumphant death is that of the

martyr. The most splendid death is that of the hero in the hour of victory. If the chariot and the horses of fire had been vouchsafed for Nelson's translation, he could scarcely have departed in a brighter blaze of glory. The most awful death is that of the martyred patriot. He has left us, not indeed his mantle of inspiration, but an example which will continue to be our shield and our strength, and a name which is our pride — an example and a name which are at this hour inspiring hundreds of the youth of England."

Which of the sentences quoted on pages 107, 108, have climax of thought?

CHAPTER VII

ON ORGANIZING THE THEME

Different Ways of Planning. — There are various kinds of composition, — description, narration, argument, and others. These will be treated one by one in later chapters. Each kind has laws of its own. Each has its own vocabulary, which may well be studied apart from other vocabularies. So, too, each type calls for special methods of organization. For the present, only a few principles of planning, applicable to all types alike, need be considered.

The Growth of a Thought. — When a thought is first conceived, it is always misty, dim, nebulous.[1] When we speak of having a " general notion," a " vague notion," we usually mean that a thought is just beginning. If it receives attention, it emerges from the nebulous condition and forms into several definite thoughts. Or, to change the figure, it

---

[1] See also Scott and Denney, *Composition-Rhetoric*, p. 72 ff. Teachers will be interested to compare an article by Miss Gertrude Buck, *Educational Review*, March, 1887. The matter is touched upon in the *History of the English Paragraph*, by the author of this book, p. 43 *et al.* (Univ. of Chicago Press).

grows and branches. Suppose that the mind awakes to the vague notion that the room is getting cold. *Cold* is the undeveloped root from which may presently branch off such thoughts as these: " Yes, it is really cold. In fact, I feel cold all over. My hands are blue, and I am shivering. Besides, Horace over there is standing with his back to the radiator, and so he too must be cold." The thought has grown into several sentences. *Cold* branched into *I am cold all over*, and this also sent off two shoots — *My hands are blue, and I am shivering.* Then the mind stopped this line of branching, and out from the stock sprang a new branch: *Horace is standing with his back to the radiator;* and then this sends off the branch *and so he too must be cold.* Try to draw a picture to represent the process that has gone on.

Now, the whole growth of a thought — stock and branches — can sometimes be expressed within the limits of one grammatical sentence. If there are too many thoughts for this, they are put into separate sentences, and the whole is called a miniature composition, or isolated paragraph.

Exactly as a paragraph grows, so a long composition may grow out of one vague idea. Some ideas have in them only enough matter to be developed into a paragraph. Others are germs from which whole books might grow. "That apple looks good" would probably develop into a short paragraph;

but, "it is strange that that apple should fall to the earth instead of away from it" might blossom into a great system of natural philosophy. If a nebulous idea has in it the making of a long theme, it will develop into main parts if the attention be fixed keenly upon it. These are paragraph nebulæ, which will subdivide into sentences. Or, to vary the figure, the main thought will send out main branches (paragraphs) which will send off lesser ones (sentences).

Unity. — Although thought grows, one must keep in mind that it does not always grow to fruit unless it is trained and pruned. Thought loves to branch, and unless restrained by a stern sense of logic, it will often end in a mere tangle of superfluous twigs and leaves. To speak less figuratively, every writer is in danger of setting down matters suggested by the subject in hand but not logically related to it. This is as true of a large piece of work as of a sentence (compare page 90). Every theme, like every sentence, should have unity. It should be the development of one idea — a large, complex idea, if you please, but, nevertheless, one. No matter how long or how short the whole, it must all concern the different phases of one thing or one thought. It should grow naturally from one germ. Every part in it should bear on the central idea of the whole — so that, after reading any given sentence, the reader can see a real connection between title and sentence. A well-organized composition cannot spare any part; each is essential to its life. Milton said, "Almost as well kill a man as kill a good book"; and we may adapt this idea to the structure of the theme. A good composition is so well organized that if you cut it anywhere it will bleed.

Planning a Paragraph. — Before writing a paragraph, try to think out the whole of it. Let the thought grow in the mind before you let it grow on paper. This method will afford a chance to review the whole mentally and to determine whether the thoughts follow each other logically.

The Topic Sentence. — When an after-dinner speaker rises to respond to a toast, he generally announces his topic at once, or after a sentence or two of introduction. He is very likely also to announce at once his chief thought about the subject; for he knows that people like to hear him come to the point. If however he has reason to think that his hearers may not agree with him immediately, he is likely to state his subject first, and then lead up gradually to his own conclusion about it.

We naturally follow some such course in writing. With each paragraph we begin a new speech, as it were. It is a matter both of courtesy and of econ-

omy if in each we state definitely what we are
talking about. The topic sentence of a paragraph
ordinarily states the general *subject,* or else declares the general *thought,* i.e. *conclusion,* of the
whole. It is generally short, because emphatic.

The following paragraph shows its general *subject* in the opening sentence.

A Tree-Planting Association has been organized in New
York City. The Association will be organized with twelve
or more members on a block, who will form a local club
under the Association. A tree-planting association may, in
this city, fail to plant trees, but it certainly will encourage
the planting of window boxes, the fencing of unused lots,
the painting of fences to the exclusion of posters, and the
general care of the public street. Back yards will assume
some relation to the general good of the community, and
trees, vines, and flowers will find place in them. The children will be taught to care for the appearance of the block
and chalk-marks and other defacements will soon disappear,
because of new-born civic pride. — *The Outlook.*

In the following paragraph, Macaulay does not
state his topic till the second sentence. The first
is a general remark by way of introduction.

One of the first objects of an inquirer, who wishes to
form a correct notion of the state of a community at a given
time, must be to ascertain of how many persons that community then consisted. *Unfortunately the population of
England in 1685, cannot be ascertained with perfect accuracy.* For no great state had then adopted the wise course
of periodically numbering the people. All men were left
to conjecture for themselves; and, as they generally con-
jectured without examining facts, and under the influence

of strong passions and prejudices, their guesses were often ludicrously absurd. Even intelligent Londoners ordinarily talked of London as containing several millions of souls. It was confidently asserted by many that, during the thirty-five years which had elapsed between the accession of Charles the First and the Restoration, the population of the City had increased by two millions. Even while the ravages of the plague and fire were recent, it was the fashion to say that the capital still had a million and a half of inhabitants. Some persons, disgusted by these exaggerations, ran violently into the opposite extreme. Thus Isaac Vossius, a man of undoubted parts and learning, strenuously maintained that there were only two millions of human beings in England, Scotland, and Ireland taken together. — MACAULAY : *History of England, Chapter III.*

In the following paragraph, the topic sentence states the general *thought* of the whole.

The appetite of this fish is almost insatiable. Mr. Jesse threw to one pike of five pounds' weight, four roach, each about four inches in length, which it devoured instantly, and swallowed[1] a fifth within a quarter of an hour. Moor-hens, ducks, and even swans have been known to fall a prey to this voracious fish, its long teeth effectually keeping them prisoners under water until drowned. — DR. J. G. WOOD.

The following paragraph states in the topic sentence the general *subject,* in the last sentence the *general thought,* which has grown out of the subject.

Two years ago the Boston School Board encouraged the establishment of cheap luncheons in the schools. Up to the

[1] Is there not some ambiguity as to the grammatical structure here ? *Swallowed* is logically the act performed by *it,* the fish, but grammatically it may be taken with —— ? Remedy the fault.

present time this has been considered an experiment.   It is now conceded that the experimental stage is passed, and that cheap, nutritious school luncheons can successfully be provided, and are in demand

The following shows how the first sentence of a paragraph may be made to include the general topic.

I cite as an instance of *the absence of vandalism in Japan* the experience of a Japanese friend of mine who lived on a street near and parallel to the busiest street in Tokio.   He had placed in his front gate, bordering immediately upon the sidewalk, an exquisite panel carved in delicate tracery and nearly two hundred years old.   Such a specimen would be placed in our Museums of Art under lock and key.   On my expressing surprise that he would expose so precious a relic without fear that some heedless boy might break off a twig, or otherwise deface it, he assured me it was quite as safe there as in his library. Three years afterwards *I* chanced to be in Japan again, and though my friend was dead, and a stranger occupied the premises, I was led to seek the place to ascertain the condition of the delicate wood-carving.   It was absolutely uninjured, though slightly bleached by the weather, and this in the great commercial city of Tokio, with a population of over one million. — EDWARD S. MORSE. [1]

Kinds of Paragraphs. — What can be said within the limits of a paragraph ?   The same things that can be said in a sentence, but more fully.   We need to consider here only a few of these.   The sentences may repeat the substance of the topic sentence, adding something new.   Or, if the paragraph states the general conclusion first, the succeeding sen-

[1] *Good Manners*, a pamphlet.   (H. L. Hastings, Boston)

tences may give the needed particulars, or illustrations, or examples, or proofs. Once more, the paragraph may open with the statement of a *cause,* this being followed by the statement of a necessary *effect.* Or, the paragraph as a whole may develop a *contrast.* Or, it may consist of a group of sentences that narrate the particulars of some event, or describe some scene.

The following paragraph exhibits a single thought by repetition.

> A true critic must love the subject-matter of literature. He must care for its message. The theme of the story, the thing the author was trying to say, must not escape him. The form of the thing is much, but the soul is more.

The following gives a general thought first, then the particulars.

> That farm bore every manner of fruit known to the climate. There were apples, a score of varieties, from the snow apple that burned among the leaves, and when bitten revealed a flesh so white that you kept biting it lest the juice should discolor it, to the great cold autumn fruits that were resonant beneath the snap of your finger. There were opulent pears, distilling the golden sun into their bottles. There were plums, the kind that succeed. Grapes there were, and quinces, and peaches, — the last not so prolific as the apples, but a very worthy fruit.

The following gives a general thought, repeats it, explains it, illustrates it, and so defends it.

> If it were only for a vocabulary, the scholar would be covetous of action. *Life* is our dictionary. Years are well

spent in country labors ; in town ; in the insight into trades and manufactures ; in frank intercourse with many men and women ; in science ; in art ; to the one end of mastering in all their facts a language by which to illustrate and embody our perceptions. I learn immediately from any speaker how much he has already lived, through the poverty or the splendor of his speech. Life lies behind us as the quarry from whence we get tiles and copestones for the masonry of to-day. This is the way to learn grammar. Colleges and books only copy the language which the field and the work-yard made. — EMERSON.

The following gives cause and effect : —

The King could not see that there were two Englands — that of himself and North, and that of Burke and Chatham. The result was inevitable. A third England sprang up across the sea.

The following sets up a quaint contrast. The passage is from Dr. Johnson's allegory on *Wit and Learning :* —

Their conduct was, whenever they desired to recommend themselves to distinction, entirely opposite. WIT was daring and adventurous ; LEARNING cautious and deliberate. WIT thought nothing reproachful but dullness ; LEARNING was afraid of no imputation but that of error. WIT answered before he understood, lest his quickness of apprehension should be questioned ; LEARNING paused, where there was no difficulty, lest any insidious sophism should lie undiscovered. WIT perplexed every debate by rapidity and confusion ; LEARNING tired the hearers with endless distinctions, and prolonged the dispute without advantage, by proving that which never was denied. WIT, in hopes of shining, would venture to produce what he had not considered, and often succeeded beyond his own expectation, by following the train of a lucky thought ; Learning would reject every new notion, for fear of being entangled in consequences which she could not foresee, and was often hindered, by her caution, from pressing her advantages, and subduing her opponent.

Oral Exercise.[1] — Each of the following paragraphs had a topic sentence stating a *cause*, which was then followed by a statement of the *effect*. Frame a topic sentence for each, stating the *cause*.

1. — — — — — — Consequently it is a good thing to apply pretty sharp tests to whatever offers itself as the genuine thing. Often the great schemes that men hatch for growing rich are nothing but pyrites. The acid of sharp common sense corrodes and discolors them.

2. — — — — — — — — — — — Nothing worse could have befallen the man. Being unused to the possession of wealth he ran through his millions in a year. In 1876 his old friend Everard met him in the street and passsed him by as a beggar.

Oral Exercise. — Examine the following paragraphs of *explanation*, and form a topic sentence for each.

1. — — — — — — — — — — — In other words, hold to the good you have. Let well enough alone. People lay great plans; they see

[1] For the idea of this exercise the author is indebted to Professors Scott and Denney, *Composition-Rhetoric* (Allyn and Bacon).

the future through rosy lenses; they build castles in Spain. But great plans that can't be carried out are of less value than small, practicable plans; the future is never just what it promises to be; and as for castles in Spain, of what value are they to owners who can neither rent nor inhabit them ?

2. — — — — — — — — — — — — It is not, observe, a mere coating of snow of given depth throughout, but it is snow loaded on until the rocks can hold no more. The surplus does not fall in the winter, because, fastened by continual frost, the quantity of snow which an Alp can carry is greater than each single winter can bestow; it falls in the first mild days of spring in enormous avalanches. Afterward the melting continues, gradually removing from all the steep rocks the small quantity of snow which was all they could hold, and leaving them black and bare among the accumulated fields of unknown depth, which occupy the capacious valleys and less inclined superficies of the mountain.

Oral Exercise. — Analyze the following narrative paragraphs from Irving's *Sketch-Book*, endeavoring to discover what office each sentence performs in the paragraph.

" We had not been long home when the sound of music was heard from a distance. A band of country lads, without coats, their shirt-sleeves fancifully tied with ribbons, their hats decorated with greens, and clubs in their hands, were seen advancing up the avenue, followed by a large number of villagers and peasantry. They stopped before the hall door, where the music struck up a peculiar air, and the lads performed a curious and intricate dance, advancing, retreating, and striking their clubs together, keeping exact time to the music; while one, whimsically crowned with a fox's skin, the tail of which flaunted down his back, kept capering round the skirts of the dance, and rattling a Christmas-box with many antic gesticulations.

" After the dance was concluded, the whole party was entertained with brawn and beef and stout home-brewed. The 'Squire himself mingled among the rustics, and was received with awkward demonstrations of deference and regard. It is true, I perceived two or three of the younger peasants, as they were raising their tankards to their mouths, when the 'Squire's back was turned, making something of a grimace, and giving each other the wink; but the moment they caught my eye they pulled grave faces, and were exceedingly demure. With Master Simon, however, they all seemed more at their ease. His varied‑occupations and amusements had made him well known throughout the neighborhood. He was a visitor at every farm-house and cottage; gossiped with the farmers and their wives; romped with their daughters; and, like that type of a vagrant bachelor, the humble-bee, tolled the sweets from all the rosy lips of the country round."

Theme. — Choose one of the following topic sentences, and develop the idea coherently, by a succession of illustrations, of details, or of particulars into a paragraph of 150 words.

1. The ghosts one hears of are not all alike.
2. In some respects, athletics are dangerous.
3. It was a dreary day.
4. It was one of those mornings that stir the blood.
5. There are battles with fate that can never be won.
6. "A dog hath his day," runs the old proverb.
7. It is easy to enumerate the ways of getting a lesson.
8. The race is not always to the swift.
9. There are many instances of bravery in everyday life.
10. Many phases of American life are illustrated in American short stories.

Theme. — Choose one of the following topic sentences, and defend it by giving reasons, proofs, to the extent of 150 or 200 words.

1. On the whole, school athletics are a good thing.

2. Vivisection is necessary to science.

3. Vivisection is cruel and unnecessary.

4. None but scientists are competent to decide whether or not vivisection is necessary to science.

5. If necessary to science, vivisection should be practised only when necessary.

6. A debating society is a help in education.

7. The American Revolution is an uninteresting theme topic.

8. The American Revolution is not an uninteresting theme topic.

[Other sentences can easily be suggested by students or teacher.]

Theme. — Develop one of the following topic sentences into a paragraph of *contrast,* — 200 words.

1. There is a difference between knowing a thing, and being able to tell it.

2. Outside the wild winds were rioting; within all was cheer.

3. I saw an old man holding his granddaughter in his arms.

4. I know two persons: one is a dreamer, the other a doer.

5. Hawthorne [or some other writer] has two characters that are strong foils to each other.

6. I imagined what was going on in those two houses.

7. Some men are always hopeful, some always in despair.

8. I knew two men of very unlike abilities.

9. I knew two persons of very unlike dispositions.

10. The great choir presented fine contrasts in color of garments.

Expansion of One Paragraph into Several. — Let it be supposed that having composed a theme of one paragraph, a student has been asked to develop the subject at greater length; the paragraph has 85 words, and the audience wants 200, or 225. What will be the right course? It is possible to expand one paragraph of 85 words into one paragraph of 225 words. But if the paragraph of 85 words has two or three distinct parts, it is better to expand each into a new paragraph.

Let it be imagined that Dr. Wood, the English naturalist, had written a very short paragraph on the Crustacea; that it ran somewhat like this.

THE CRUSTACEA

The aquatic animals known as the Crustacea have no internal skeleton, but are defended by a strong crust, made of a series of rings. This unyielding armor, together with the coverings of the eyes, the tendons of the claws, and the lining membrane of the stomach, with its teeth, is cast off annually to permit the growth of the body. The Crustacea possess the power of reproducing a lost or original limb; and, indeed, if injured the animal itself shakes off the injured joint.

Suppose, now, that Dr. Wood found himself dissatisfied with these somewhat cramped and overloaded sentences, and determined to rewrite, making three paragraphs where he had formerly but one. In the new theme, the main topics would be, as before: *Definition of Crustacea; Annual shedding; Reproduction of Limbs.* Each would have a paragraph to itself, where before it had but a sentence. All the sentences to be made about the Definition would be set off by themselves as one main part of the theme; all those about the Shedding would form a second; all those about the New Limbs, a third.

"Set off"; — that is, by *indentation,* or *indention.* This word means, "a biting in," or, more properly "a biting out." Where a new division of the theme begins, the first line does not come up plumb to the straight edge at the left; it is bitten into; it begins farther to the right than do the other lines. In the printed book, the indentation is small — usually the width of a letter *m.* But in a manuscript it is important for the indentation to be absolutely unmistakable. Some persons keep so ragged an edge at the left hand that it is impossible to know whether or not they should be credited with understanding what a paragraph is. Indent each new paragraph one or two inches. Bring every line of the paragraph, *except the last,* up even with the right-hand margin; the last line may be stopped

K

anywhere, if the paragraph is complete in sense; often this line has but a word or two. If at any time you inadvertently omit the indentation, and have not time to copy, place a paragraph mark where the new paragraph should begin; thus, ¶.

A rough outline for Dr. Wood's new paragraphs could now be made. The topics being known, the number of sentences under each could be guessed at. There is nothing in the original paragraph to show that Dr. Wood ascribed especial importance to some one of the three topics. The third is perhaps the least important. It may be estimated that in the completed theme he would give about 80 words to each of the first two, and about 50 to the third. The outline would be something like this, the full stops representing those of the future theme.

The Crustacea

¶ Crustacea are aquatic. No skeleton, but crust, which protects and strengthens. Framework of rings ; part develops into limbs. Articulated animals.

¶ Curious way of growth. Other animals not inconvenienced as they grow. Not so Crustacea. Mail unyielding. Is cast off annually and larger coat grows. Eye-covering, tendons, stomach-membrane are also shed.

¶ Curious reproduction of lost or injured limb. New one grows if old lost ; animal shakes off injured joint. Lobsters do, when alarmed.

As a matter of fact, Dr. Wood did write a short chapter on the Crustacea, and here it is.

The Crustacea

The Crustacea are almost all aquatic animals. They have no internal skeleton, but their body is covered with a strong crust, which serves for protection as well as for strength. Their whole framework consists of a series of rings fitted to, and working in each other ; some forming limbs, and others developing into the framework supporting the different organs. From this reason, they and the remaining animals, as far as the star-fishes, who have no limbs at all, are called "articulated" animals.

Their method of growth is very curious. Other animals as they increase in size, experience no particular inconvenience. Not so the Crustacea. Their bodies are closely enveloped in a strong, unyielding mail, which cannot grow with them. Their armor is therefore cast off every year, and a fresh coat formed to suit their increased dimensions Not only is the armor cast off, but even the covering of the eyes, the tendons of the claws, and the lining membrane of the stomach, with its teeth.

They all also possess the curious power of reproducing a lost or injured limb. In the former case, a fresh limb supplies the place of that lost ; and in the latter case, the animal itself shakes off the injured joint, and a new one soon takes its place. Lobsters, when alarmed, frequently throw off their claws.

Theme. — Choose one of the following paragraphs and expand it into a theme. Each sentence should grow into a paragraph. The proportions to be observed are suggested by the number of amplifying sentences prescribed for the different paragraphs. Write a title above the theme.

1. (*a*) I like winter for its outdoor sports. [Four

or five sentences.] (*b*) I like it no less for its in-door sports. [Four or five sentences.]

2. (*a*) Wearing birds is foolish, for it is a rem-nant of savagery, like tattooing. [Two or three sentences.] (*b*) It is less artistic than is often supposed. [Two or three sentences.] (*c*) It is unwise, because it threatens the extinction of cer-tain species of flycatchers and warblers. [Two or three sentences.] (*d*) It is cruel, necessitating slaughter of innocent life, and producing callous-ness to suffering. [Five or six sentences.]

3. (*a*) A contrast between faces. [Two sen-tences.] (*b*) The face of Napoleon is intellectual firm, and cruel. [Three sentences, giving details of the face.] (*c*) The face of Lincoln is intellectual, firm, and kind. [Three sentences, giving details.]

4. (*a*) There are two kinds of people, — those who know what they want life to do for them, and those who do not. [This introductory sentence may be made a part of the first paragraph.] The people who know what they want are few. [Three or four sentences.] (*b*) The people who do not know what they want are partly young people, who have not had training enough to know; partly older people. [Three or four sentences.]

5. (*a*) Some dinners I like, some I do not. [Part of first paragraph.] The kinds I like; food; company. [Three or four sentences.] The kinds I do not like; food; company. [Three or four sentences.]

Oral Exercise. — Discuss with the instructor and the class the best way of paragraphing each of the following topics. Form first an idea as to how many paragraphs each should have and what should be the paragraph subjects. 1. This recitation room. 2. How Lincoln looked. 3. A painting I like. 4. What I do in a day. 5. My plans. 6. The walk to school. 7. My past education. 8. The elm. 9. The construction of the steam engine. 10. An ocean steamer. 11. Evening in the country.

Oral Exercise. — Read carefully the following speech and state the paragraph subjects. Estimate the number of words in each paragraph, and say whether you think the proportion of parts is bad or good. The speech will be recognized as that delivered by Lincoln at the dedication of the Gettysburg National Cemetery. It was written first as one paragraph; but a year later, in making a copy, the President divided it as you see.

"Fourscore and seven years ago, our fathers brought forth on this continent a new nation, conceived in liberty, and dedicated to the proposition that all men are created equal.

"Now we are engaged in a great civil war, testing whether that nation, or any nation so conceived and so dedicated, can long endure. We are met on a great battlefield of that war. We have come to dedicate a portion of that field as a final resting-place for those who here gave their lives that that nation might live. It is altogether fitting and proper that we should do this.

" But, in a larger sense, we cannot dedicate — we cannot consecrate — we cannot hallow this ground. The brave men, living and dead, who struggled here, have consecrated it far above our poor power to add or detract. The world will little note, nor long remember, what we say here, but it can never forget what they did here. It is for us, the living, rather to be dedicated here to the unfinished work which they who fought here have thus far so nobly advanced. It is rather for us to be here dedicated to the great task remaining before us — that from these honored dead we take increased devotion to that cause for which they gave the last full measure of devotion, — that we here highly resolve that these dead shall not have died in vain, — that this nation, under God, shall have a new birth of freedom, — and that government of the people, by the people, for the people, shall not perish from the earth."

Oral Exercise. — The importance of modelling all work on the right scale is illustrated in the task of the editor of an encyclopædia. His problem is to give each subject space and prominence according to its importance. Opening Johnson's

Encyclopædia, I find seven columns devoted to Shakespeare. Of these, two and a half are given to the poet's life, four and a half to his works. Is the proportion about right? If you were editing an encyclopædia of geography, how much space should you give to Africa as compared with Europe? How much, if the encyclopædia dealt with civilization?

Oral Exercise in Proportioning.—In treating each of the following subjects, (*a*) what paragraph topics might be chosen? (*b*) which paragraph ought to be the longest, dealing with the most important phase of the subject? 1. Living statesmen. 2. Advantages of country life. 3. The life of Lincoln. 4. The uses of gold. 5. A railway accident. 6. A cyclone. 7. A visit to an art-gallery. 8. A week of camping.

Exercise in Varying the Scale.— Read one of the following poems. Then write two papers, the first retelling (not closely paraphrasing) the story of the poem in one paragraph of about 100 words, the second retelling the same story in a theme of 300 words, properly paragraphed. *In each theme give space to every part according to its relative importance.*

Browning: Tray — about vivisection; Clive — story of courage; Incident of the French camp — story of heroism; How we brought the good news from Ghent to Aix — story of endurance; The Pied

Piper of Hamelin — story of pathos; Muleykeh —
owner's pride in a horse; The Bean Feast — a
Pope's humility. Longfellow: The Bell of Atri;
Paul Revere's Ride; Evangeline; The Legend
Beautiful; Robert of Sicily. Lowell: The Vision
of Sir Launfal. Drayton: The Ballad of Agincourt
(*Heart of Oak Books*, Vol. V.). Thackeray: Chron-
icle of the Drum (*Ibid.*). Tennyson: The Revenge
(*Ibid.*). Coleridge: The Rime of the Ancient
Mariner (*Ibid.*). Whittier: Skipper Ireson's Ride
(*Ibid.*).

Choice of Topic; Method of Work. — It is easier
to choose among definite theme subjects, printed in
the book, than to choose from an unlimited number
of topics. Left free, a person may be attracted to
a subject that is either too large, or else mechani-
cally limited. The latter kind is the easier to
manage. "The parts of a certain city," is a topic
easily paragraphed. To choose no subjects but
such as this would lead a person into making his
theme in water-tight compartments. On the other
hand, what can any one write in half an hour that
will interest a reasonable being in such a subject
as Water, or Clouds, or Steam, or Electricity, or
the Rise and Fall of Nations?

If the student is given free choice of a subject,
he should select something that he really cares
about, and that he wishes some definite audience

to care about.   Different modes of treatment are necessary to interest different audiences.

Very often the attractive subject will not be capable of easy analysis.   In such a case, choose only a few paragraph topics, thus narrowing the treatment; pick out the most attractive phases of the subject.

This done, invent a theme title that will give an adequate hint of what is coming.   The actor, Mr. Joseph Jefferson, once made a charming talk to some college men about the "starring system," concluding with remarks about the fancy of some people that Bacon wrote Shakespeare and put a cryptogram into the plays.   A college periodical, wanting to give some hint of both topics, reported the speech under the heading "Stars and Cryptograms."   It was not a very good title, for it was meaningless.   But it was designed to rouse curiosity, and, taken in connection with Jefferson's name, it did as well, I dare say, as a less vague and fanciful title.

Let it be supposed that a person is to choose a subject for a simple theme, — any subject he pleases.   He is to select one that will interest high school students as well as himself.   His window looks out on a lake.   How will *Lakes* do, for a topic?   It is too large; one would never have done. Nobody enjoys reading a small theme on a large matter.   The window affords a glimpse of the lake;

perhaps this *Glimpse of the Lake* would serve for a theme. There would be no difficulty in paragraphing; one section would go to the water, one to the boats, one to the sky. But the water would have to be described exactly as it now looks, though looking its worst. The boats are all absent except one, and perhaps there are other kinds that he would like to tell about. Besides, the lad in the boat is fishing, and the writer may be glad to tell about the fishing on this lake. If however memories of the past few days must be dragged in to make the theme interesting to us all, why, the name must be changed. The writer may call it, *A Glimpse of the Lake and Some Memories;* the title can then be interpreted with some elasticity.

What, now, are the chief things to say? A brief paragraph of introduction, perhaps, though that is by no means necessary. Then something about the look of the lake. Then a word about the boats. Then something about the fishing. Here is enough: *water, boats, fishing.*

Now for the outline. ¶ Sprained ankle, armchair. Must study landscape. Window shows lake. ¶ Lake has moods. Dull now. Glare this morning, colors last night. Sometimes calm; crystal depths. Ripples. Wind makes it blossom; raises undercurrents. Rain quiets it. Freckled look. Queer way water *fits* land. ¶ Steamer seen. Variety of boats. Red-stack boats. Swarms of passengers. Boats gay at night. Launches. Pulse of engines. Sailboat. It upset, the other day. Rowboats. Fisherman. ¶ Casting for bass. Amateur. Wish him luck! I tried for pike. Tried for bass. No luck. Tried for perch. Caught a bass. [Six or eight sentences.]

In the last paragraph it perhaps occurs to the writer that the bullheads bite when the water is muddy; and this *muddiness* suggests the first paragraph; the *muddiness* should be described back there with the changing look of the water.

Next, the composition. It is not offered as a model of style, but to suggest a possible way of organizing any simple theme.

A Glimpse of the Lake, and Some Memories

Here I am, planted in an armchair before the window, my sprained ankle reposing, or trying to repose, on a smaller chair. In such a position one must be thankful for his mercies; he must take the exceptional chance to study the landscape. Fortunately, the window cuts off a goodly section of the lake which lies down there below.

An exquisite thing is the lake, with as many moods as a baby. Just now it is dull in color, for the sky is overcast and there is mist in the air. But early this morning it blazed with light, and last night at sunset it was awake with every fashion of color. Sometimes, when the heavens are bare and windless, the water takes on an indescribable calm; and then if you look down from this height there seems to be no surface at all — only depths of blue, such as the poets are always likening to crystal or to sapphire. At other times clouds and a breeze move over it, and the surface ruffles till one's mind is tired with fancying the million lines of ripples. If the wind stiffens and stays by, there soon are waves ; the water breaks white and springs up in blossoms over the whole dark field ; then the under streams are roused out of their quiet and the whole mass thunders in upon the shore, muddy but grand. Now it begins to rain ; and rain is the witch that charms the savage waters into rest. Presently the surface is dull again, but for the freckled look made by the plunging drops. One notes through the gathering mist an odd thing — the way the water seems to settle into place, fitting into the curves and nooks of the shore ; the edge of the lake seems to grow white and distinct, and to cling to the land in a sharp outline.

Breaking through that white streak of water near the shore comes a dark something, which soon takes form and is seen to be a steamer. What a variety of craft haunt the lake ! The largest are these tall steamers, taller still for their red stacks. At night, with their colored lights, they look like jewelled slippers. By day they carry crowds, which seem to rim each deck with a black band. Then there are the launches, slipping here and there straight across the bow of the bigger craft. They have a curiously trim and self-satisfied look ; and their naphtha engines, beating no louder than some great, fast pulse, seem to make fun of the slow-puffing monsters that stain the air with smoke. A sailboat — a little sloop — slips across the picture. It is the one that upset the other day and gave my friend the Doctor a thorough soaking. Two rowboats are standing to the south. In the bow of one there's a lone fisherman.

That lad is casting for bass. He is an amateur — from his dress. Better luck to him than has thus far befallen the amateur who sits watching him from this window! *I* trolled in the lake for silver pike, but with never a rise to break the monotony. Then *I* tried thrice in the early morning for yellow bass, using first minnows for bait, afterward grasshoppers, and lastly frogs. No luck ! Disgusted, *I* stole out one afternoon to catch perch, hoping to be seen by no one.

The perch bit languidly, and the few that were taken seemed to have a supercilious look. "Here's my last worm!" I cried; "then for the hotel and farewell to these fishing grounds where no fish are." A bite! a competent, masterly, vicious bite! It's a bass, strayed away from home, and too hungry to ask for delicate diet! Pull him in — seize the line, for the pole is light and the hook is small. Safely landed, and not less in weight than two pounds! Let them brag of six-pounders; this gleaming, muscular fellow, smelling of fresh water and mint, is good enough game for me. As *I* gaze and remember, the amateur in his boat moves out of the picture frame and the lake is a blank again.

Oral Exercise. — Why are the following subjects unfit for short themes? Suggest two or three theme topics that might be derived from each. 1. George Washington. 2. Snow. 3. War. 4. Evening. 5. Light. 6. Politeness.

Oral Exercise. — Name several limited subjects that would be available if you were trying to interest legitimately (*a*) an audience of college men, (*b*) an audience of high school boys, (*c*) an audience of high school girls, (*d*) an audience of business men.

Theme. — Choose one of the following subjects, and think how to secure for it the interest of persons three or four years younger than yourself. Think of some intelligent boy or girl, one who, though considerably your junior, distinctly commands your respect, and explain to him high school ways of studying either (*a*) physiography, or (*b*) history, or (*c*) Latin, or (*d*) manual training, or (*e*) English, or some other subject. The theme should consist of one paragraph, of about 200 words.

Oral and Written Exercise. — Choose *three* of the following subjects, and think what illustrations you would use to make them clear to different audiences. Draw upon your knowledge of the things that are most familiar to the experience of each audience. Jot down memoranda of the illustrations that you suggest, and afterward compare notes in the oral discussion. For example,

Explain, by illustration : —

A gentleman, to a gamin.

Ice, to a native of the tropics.

The charm of foot-ball, to a girl.

The pleasure of work, to a shirk.

Wagner's music, to a deaf painter.

The charm of foot-ball, to a soldier.

The solar system, to a child of eight.

Oranges, to a native of the polar regions.

The charm of a true lady, to an awkward lad.

The Jungle Book, to a North American Indian.

A newsboy's life, to an earl's son or a millionnaire's son.

A sleepless night, to a person who sleeps like a top.

A headache, to a person who never had a headache.

The charm of Stevenson, to a reader of dime novels.

Taking gas at the dentist's, to a person who never lost a tooth.

An encyclopædia, to a man who never heard of such a book.

Paragraph construction, to a youth who cares only for the shop.

The danger of open windows, to a child who never heard of death.

Some good monthly, to a bright boy or girl who had never seen a magazine.

Transitions between Paragraphs. — Suppose that a given theme is a unit, no idea being admitted that does not bear on the topic; suppose, further, that the paragraphs are units, each treating a distinct part of the theme idea; it remains to be sure that the reader gets easily from paragraph to paragraph. Sometimes the writer is so anxious to make each paragraph a unit in itself that the reader does not feel at once that the new section has anything to do with the preceding.

Look back to the theme on the *Glimpse of the Lake.* There were three things to talk about · water, boats, fishing. At the end of the paragraph on *the water* the attention must be led over without any jar to the subject of *boats.* The last idea of the *water* paragraph was that the edge of the lake grew white and distinct. In beginning the new paragraph, we may refer to that idea. ˙ "Breaking through that white streak of water near the shore comes a dark something," etc.

Now look at the paragraph on fishing. How does the writer try to get over to the *fishing* from the *boats* ? Explain in recitation.

The joints of the theme should be smooth and strong, like the joints of bamboo — not a rude joint made by chisel and hammer.

Written Exercise. — The instructor will hand you in class your themes thus far written. Go over them carefully, trying by revision to make the thought connection closer between the paragraphs. For the future, always read carefully the whole paragraph before beginning the next.

Transitions between Sentences. — Within the paragraph each sentence should grow vitally out of the preceding. "Connection is the soul of good writing," said the great translator, Jowett of Balliol. *Plan sentences ahead ; and read each sentence before you write the next.* Make it impossible for people to say of you as they used to say of Emerson, "His sentences read equally well in any order." Make it impossible to pick a sentence out and set it down elsewhere, without tearing the theme as Æneas rent young Polydore.

Frequently the sentences can be bound tighter

together by beginning the next with a reference to some idea contained in the preceding. Burke, pleading in Parliament for America, said: "But with regard to her own internal establishment, she may, I doubt not she will, contribute in moderation. I say in moderation, for she ought not to be permitted to exhaust herself. She ought to be reserved to a war, the weight of which, with the enemies that we are most likely to have, must be considerable in her quarter of the globe. There she may serve you, and serve you essentially." Here the last words of each sentence suggest the first words of the next. Of course this way of getting coherence is easily overdone; but it is very valuable, nevertheless.

It is easy to discover the order in which Ruskin wrote the following sentences, here printed in wrong order. Find the true arrangement, and tell how it was found.

Well, whatever bit of a wise man's work is honestly and benevolently done, that bit is his book, or his piece of art. But, again, I ask you, do you at all believe in honesty or at all in kindness, or do you think there is never any honesty or benevolence in wise people? If you read rightly you will easily discover the true bits, and those *are* the book.

Oral Exercise. — Change either the grammatical construction or the order of words wherever you think such change will increase the coherence of the following paragraph.

" We were coasting down chapel hill.   In western New York, this is one of many similar long hills. This state is indeed a coaster's paradise in many parts.   The particular paradise I speak of, saw, however, a disastrous fall of a brave young Adam and a gentle young Eve.   Williams, I mean by this, who was coming like a meteor down the hill, with Miss —— in front of him on the " bob-sled," as he reached the bridge, was thrown out of the track.   Luckless bridge! it ought to have been guarded by stout rails.   There were no rails, however, and across the narrow canyon, Williams, with his precious charge, took a flying leap.   On the other side of it, five feet below, was a wooden abutment.   The lives of the young people were saved by this; for the sled shot across the gulf and landed on the projection.   We picked the adventurers up from this perilous perch.   They were more surprised than hurt.   But after he had time to think, Williams confessed that he was never more frightened in his life; for he thought of the thirty feet of space below that wooden ledge."

CHAPTER VIII

ON CORRECTNESS IN CHOICE OF WORDS

Authority. — If the art of writing is the art of saying what we mean, we must use words that the reader will understand. Of course the word *reader* is rather general: there are readers and readers. An article written for adults would show different words from one written for children. For the purposes of this chapter, our typical reader is the American or the Englishman who has a good public school training. This "average man" may in theory happen to live in London, or in Maine, or, again, in Texas. Now, there are certain words used in Texas that are not used in London or in Maine. In parts of New Jersey and Pennsylvania a small pail is called a "blickey." Most natives of Chicago never heard the word. Such words as "blickey" are called *provincialisms* or *localisms*, and are ruled out. Our words must be *national*. This need not mean international; many words are used in England that need not be used in America, and *vice versâ*. The American speaks of *switching* a train; the Englishman

147

speaks of *shunting* it. With the former the train goes up a steep *grade;* with the latter it goes up a *gradient.* The Englishman calls *baggage, luggage,* a word that Americans are more likely to use of those pieces only that can be carried in the hand. It is to be presumed that national differences of this sort are known to American and Englishman alike; therefore there is no reason why either should change from the usage of his country. Good English is essentially the same in all English-speaking countries.

One other matter is suggested by the words *national usage.* A nation is composed of all sorts and conditions of men. Each class, each trade and profession, has its own pet expressions and contractions. Good usage does not recognize these. The dialect of the college, or the ball-ground, or the counting-room, or the law-courts, is racy enough and proper enough in its place; but it has no place in standard English. A student may *flunk*, but only in school. A book of accounts can be *posted,* but not a man.

Again, our words must not be so old-fashioned or obsolete that they are unintelligible. They must be *present. Let* once meant "to hinder." Naturally no one would use it in this sense to-day.

Many words that are both national and present are not permitted, since they are not *reputable.* They are used, but wrongly so; used by the careless and the uneducated. A great number of such expressions are perfectly well understood wherever English is spoken, but if one employs them one will be set down as careless or ignorant; for example, *ain't* is intelligible to all, but its use is known to be a mark of vulgarity; such a word is called a *vulgarism*. Most slang consists of vulgarisms, though some slang finally becomes reputable English. Reputable words are those employed by the best writers. By *best* is meant writers who have literary distinction, and who know and regard the structure and history of English literary words. In this day, when everybody scribbles and prints, there are countless writers whose usage is not really reputable. The newspapers, though they have done much to free modern English from pedantry, are not usually reputable in usage. The English of very many novelists is in bad repute. Even certain writers of eminence, such as Dickens and Thomas Hughes, are guilty of using unreputable words and senses of words. Such essayists as Matthew Arnold and John Fiske; such writers of fiction as Thackeray, Hawthorne, Stevenson, and Henry James; such historians as Green and Parkman — these men are in general safe models in matters of usage.

To sum up, then; if we would be understood, and would be reckoned as educated persons, we must use words that are reputable, national, and present.

Good usage is the employment of such words and senses of words as the body of reputable writers sanction by their own practice to-day. Notice that *the body* of reputable writers is specified. No one author makes good use, any more than one swallow makes a summer. When a critic wishes to prove by authority that a given expression is English, he must be able to quote it from many authors.

The Dictionary. — A dictionary is a codification of good usage. Indeed, a large dictionary codifies also much bad usage, explaining in the case of the latter the particular form of badness, whether local usage, or colloquial usage, or vulgar usage. Such a dictionary also outlines the history of each word, so far as this is known; it can here be learned what was standard English yesterday, what three centuries ago. A dictionary habit is indispensable to every one. When in doubt about the present meaning or pronunciation of a word, or curious as to its history, look it up. Have an abridged dictionary of your own, — the less abridged the better, — but consult also the unabridged books frequently. Every author rediscovers the charm that lies in the dictionary. To find that charm, every word of the given explanations should be read, and the system of *diacritical marks*, which show syllabification, accent, vowel, and consonant sounds, should be studied.

Barbarisms. — Lord Chesterfield writes to his son: "The first thing you should attend to is, to speak whatever language you do speak, in its greatest purity, and according to the rules of grammar; for we must never offend against grammar, nor make use of words which are not really words."

A word that is not in a good dictionary, or is there branded as provincial or as vulgar, is not really a word, and should not be used. An expression that has not been recognized by good use is called a *barbarism*. Often such terms are incorrectly formed, as when they are coined by ignorant persons; often they are corruptions of words. *Motorneer* is wrongly coined; *slick* is corrupted from *sleek*. *Motorneer* is made up of *motor* plus the ending *er*. The *ne* is left over from the discarded steam engine, for *motorneer* is made by false analogy from *engineer*. The proper word is *motorman*. If there is need for a new word in the language, — and the need often arises in these days of invention, — its component parts should be from the same tongue, and it should be formed by strict analogy, on the model of some correct, accepted word. Examine such a word as *shadowgraph*, which the more careless newspapers began to use as soon as the "Roentgen rays" were discovered. *Shadow* is English; *graph* is Greek, — a termination that should be added only to a Greek word. Various correct formations have been proposed for the ray-picture — *scotograph, radiograph, skiagraph,* etc. It remains to be seen which one of these words will become established. Examine the word *electrocution.* It is formed on the false analogy of *execution. Execution* is from the Latin *ex + sequor,* meaning "to follow up," or, so to speak, "to chase down" The man who invented *electrocution* could not have known that *sequor* was a part of *execution.* He merely tied together *electro* and *cution,* thinking perhaps that *cution* meant cutting or killing. *Electro* is from the Greek (meaning "amber," the substance by rubbing which some one discovered electricity), and in strictness should not be joined to a Latin termination, even if that be correct. We might easily have had a good English word for death in the electrical chair; but as matters stand, there is no one recognized word for this idea.

Other barbarisms are: *burglarize, to enthuse* (a bad coinage from *enthusiasm), an invite, double entendre* and *nom de plume* (two expressions which are neither accepted French nor accepted English), *walkist, a combine, preventative* (for *preventive), reportorial, managerial, to suicide, gent, pants* (the trade name, but not the literary), *photo, praf, spoonsful.* Words brought into the English from other languages, and not yet recognized by good use, are also barbarisms. Such words are said to be not yet *Anglicized.* They are referred to as *alienisms,* and most may be classified as Latinisms, Hellenisms (or Greek words), Teutonisms (chiefly German words), Gallicisms (French words). A word peculiar to America is an *Americanism;* one peculiar to England is a *Briticism.* Some Americanisms and Briticisms are not really barbarisms, but are warranted by the canon of national use.

The following words are as yet alienisms: *artiste, sobriquet, beau monde, faux pas, entre nous,* etc. Certain other words are Anglicized: *amateur, omelette, etiquette, litterateur,* etc. The temptation to sprinkle foreign words unnecessarily into one's English reaches most persons sooner or later. It should be withstood. The English language is rich enough to furnish forth any man's vocabulary.

Many words that may finally become good English are not yet accepted. To be on the safe side one should say: *point of view,* not *standpoint; upon,* not *onto; written permission,* not *a permit; he doesn't,* not *he don't.*[1]

In the list given above it is remarked of *pants* that it is a trade name (for what are ordinarily known as trousers or pantaloons). Commercial English and literary English are two different things; and while a careful novelist would hardly write about *wheatena,* or *flexibone,* or *autoharp,* he might talk about them in the shops. Yet these words are not correctly formed; and the same thing is unhappily true of other trade names.

[1] See however *do, does,* in the Oxford English Dictionary.

Improprieties. — Suppose, now, that a writer uses a good English word, but uses it in a sense not found in the best authors. In this case he uses the word improperly; he commits an *impropriety*. Sometimes two words sound so much alike that they are mistaken one for the other; for instance, *accept* and *except*. Sometimes the two words mean nearly the same thing, and so come to be confused; for example, *continual* and *continuous*. The following list gives the words that are most frequently mistaken for each other. In the illustrative sentences each such word is correctly used, and in all cases the other word would be incorrect or at least less desirable if substituted for it.

NOUNS

Ability, capacity.

1. The *capacity* of man's memory is great.
2. *Capacity* for learning and *ability* for doing are secrets of success.

What idea do these words share?

Acceptance, acceptation.

1. His *acceptance* was graceful.
2. You use the word in its usual *acceptation*.

Each of these words contains the idea to *take*. In what sense may this be said?

Access, accession.

1. *Access* to the director is easy.

2. The library has received an *accession* of books.

3. She was seized with an *access* of grief.

4. The Tsar celebrated his *accession* to the throne.

Each of these words contains the idea of *entrance*. *Access* means the entrance of a person into a room or into the presence of another; also the entrance of a flood of emotion into the mind. *Accession* means the entrance of a person into the rights of a position; also the entrance of books or other objects to a collection, — an addition to the collection.

Act, action.

1. Character is developed by *action*.

2. Our own *acts* for good or ill speak for us.

Explain how both these words hold the idea of *do*.

Advance, advancement.

1. The swallow comes with the *advance* of the season.

2. He has received *advancement*.

3. Each *advance* of Napoleon was swift.

What idea have these two words in common? Explain how they differ.

Alternative, choice.

1. There is no *alternative;* he must go.

2. There are only three *choices*.

Alternative is a choice between —— things.

Avocation, vocation.

1. My regular calling, or *vocation*, is teaching; but for an *avocation* I spend my holidays in photography.

2. Dr. Weir Mitchell is a physician; but his regular *vocation* of medicine doesn't prevent him from following the delightful *avocation* of letters.

Both these words have the idea of *calling*. Explain how they differ. (What does *ab* mean in Latin?)

Balance, remainder.

1. The *balance* of the sum is due.

2. The *remainder* of the day is spent.

What relation exists between *balancing* (*a book*) and *remainder?*

Character, reputation.

1. His r*eputation* for integrity is good.

2. His *character* is beyond reproach.

3. A man cannot always control his *reputation*, but he can control his *character*.

Character is what a man ——; reputation is what people —— of him.

Compliment, complement.

1. Woman's mind is by many considered the *complement* of man's, supplying certain things that the masculine mind has not.

2. His *compliments* are really *flatteries*.

3. The secretary supplied the army with its *complement* of stores.

Council, counsel.

1. His *counsel* defended him in the trial.
2. Let good *counsel* prevail.
3. The *council* of ten gave good *counsel*.

Define these two words. What idea have they in common?

Falseness, falsity.

Arnold was a traitor; and the *falseness* of his character was proved by the *falsity* of his statements.

What idea do these words share? Frame definitions.

Invention, discovery.

Edison *discovered* certain laws of sound and by them *invented* the phonograph. This *invention* is not as yet very useful; but the *discovery* of the laws was important.

What idea do these words share? Frame definitions.

Limit, limitation.

1. There should be no *limitation* of the commander's authority.
2. There were no *limits* to his delight.

What common idea have these words? Define each.

Majority, plurality.

A *majority* is more than half the whole number. A *plurality* is the excess of votes received by one candidate above another. When there are several candidates, the one who receives more votes than any other has a plurality.

In what respect are these words alike in meaning? in what unlike?

Observation, observance.

1. His *observation* of the habits of birds was keen.
2. His *observance* of the Sabbath was strict.

Is *watch* the best word for the idea shared by these words? Discuss.

Observation, remark.

1. Johnson's *observations* of men were keen.
2. Johnson's *observations* were made with his eyes; his *remarks*, with his tongue; and Boswell, by recording the remarks, recorded the *observations*.

What relation has a *remark* to an *observation?*

Party, person.

1. A *party* in a silk hat must be a party of Liliputians.
2. The *party* of the first part was two *persons*.
3. A seedy *person* joined the *party*.
4. I refuse to be a *party* to the deed.

Is the idea of a *part* always contained in the word *party?* Discuss.

Part, portion.

1. Esau sold his *portion*, the part allotted him.
2. The human body has many *parts*.
3. Waiter, one *portion* of roast beef will do !

What is a *portion?*

Prominent, predominant.

There were many *prominent* men in Lincoln's cabinet, but the President was always *predominant* among them.

Consult the unabridged as to the origin of these words.

Recipe, receipt.

If *receipt* comes from the Latin meaning " taken," it is easy to see why when money is taken a *receipt* is given. *Recipe* is a Latin imperative, meaning "take"; naturally it is the right word for a formula in cooking; "take" so much salt, so much meal so much water — and lo ! a johnny cake.

Relative, relation.

One may have many *relatives* with whom he does not keep up close *relations*.

Is *relation* preferably an abstract noun, or a concrete ?

Residence, house.

1. Do not say *residence* when you mean house ·
the simpler word is the better.

2. He has his *residence* in his house.

3. His *residence*, or place of *residence*, is Montreal.

Sewage, sewerage.

The *sewage* flows through the system of *sewerage*.

Site, situation.

1. Lovely is Zion for *situation*.

2. The *site* of Troy was repeatedly built upon, each new Troy being in turn destroyed by fire or by some enemy.

3. The *situation* of Chicago by the lake gives the city fresh breezes.

What kind of place is a *site?* What is a *situation?*

VERBS

Accept, except.

1. All Cretans are liars, runs the proverb: the proverb *excepts* none.

2. He *accepted* the invitation.

Both words have the idea of *take.* How is this true of *except?*

Affect, effect.

1. Even the rumor *affected* his belief, changing it slightly.

2. He *effected* a junction with the other army.

Which of these words could properly govern *reconciliation? mind? health? release? conduct after release? destruction? conscience? peace of mind?* Which one of the two words requires for an object a noun expressing an action?

Aggravate, irritate, tantalize.

1. Tantalus was *tantalized* by the sight of inaccessible fruit.

2. He *aggravates* the difficulty by trying to excuse his act.

3. He is *aggravating* his cold by going out.

4. He *irritates* me by his teasing.

5. The gravity of our case is but *aggravated* by delay.

Allude, mention.

1. Nobody would *allude* to an experience so unpleasant to all that party.

2. He *alluded* to Washington as the Father of his Country.

3. He *mentioned* several ways of accomplishing the work; then he went back to his duties, not *alluding* to the subject again.

Can a person *allude* to a thing without assuming knowledge of it on the part of an audience? Can a thing be *alluded* to for the first time? if so, would it be the first time it was spoken of? Make *allusions* to several great men without *mentioning* their names.

M

Antagonize, alienate.

1. By *antagonizing* the views of his friends, he *alienated* their sympathies from him.

2. He *alienated* his friends by *antagonizing* them.

Begin, commence.

These words are often interchangeable, but *commence* is the more formal.   *Begin* is the better word ordinarily.

Bring, fetch.

1. Come here and *bring* the book.

2. Go and *fetch* the book.

Define these two words.   What is their common idea?

Claim, assert, etc.

1. *Claim* means to assert a right to a thing as one's own.   It means neither *to say, to assert, to declare, to maintain, to hold, to allege,* nor *to contend.*

2. He *claims* the right to be heard.

3. He *maintains* that he ought to be heard.

4. He *asserts* that such is the fact.

Note. — It is better not to use *claim* with the conjunction *that.*

Degrade, demean, debase.

1. Being in disgrace, the captain was *degraded* from his rank.

2. He *demeans* himself sometimes well, sometimes ill.

3. He *debases* [or *degrades*] himself by his profanity.

Give a synonym for *demean.*

Drive, ride.

In England one *rides* only when one is on horseback; one is said to *drive* if in a carriage. In America one *drives* when one holds the reins; but we *go driving* even when the coachman drives. There is also excellent authority for *take a ride,* and *go riding,* when conveyance in a carriage is meant.

Endorse, approve, second.

1. He *seconded* all his friend's propositions.
2. He *endorsed* the check across the top.
3. He *approved* his colleague's act.

What is a *dorsal* fin? What does *endorse* mean, by etymology?

Got, gotten, have.

1. *Got* is perhaps preferable to *gotten.*
2. Don't say you've *got* a thing when you merely *have it,* without having secured it.

What idea is common to *get* and *have?*

Guess, think, reckon.

1. I *think* I shall go.
2. He *reckoned* the cost before he started.

3. I *guess* there are a hundred.

[The habitual misuse of *guess* is an American fault.]

Intend, calculate.

1. She received his apologies with a resentment they were *likely*, but were not intended, to inspire.[1]

2. He aimed at the animal a blow *calculated* to kill it.

3. I fully *intend* to go, but cannot *calculate* how soon.

Let, leave.

1. *Let* me be! Don't bother me when I want to study.

2. *Let* me alone!

3. *Leave* me alone here.

4. *Let* go! Unhand me.

Let once meant "to hinder." Now it means the opposite — "permit."

Lie, lay.

The chief trouble with the first of these two words seems to concern the past tense: "He *laid down* on the sofa."

Locate, settle.

1. He *located his house* there (not *located there*).

2. He *settled* in Chicago.

---

[1] A. S. Hill: *Foundations of Rhetoric*, p. 110 (Harper's).

Loan, lend.

It is not incorrect to use *loan* in the sense of *lend*, but *lend* is the less formal and the preferable word.

May, can.

May it not be said that any person who has not learned the difference between these two words, *can* hardly be permitted to call himself a user of good English?

It is not hard to see why people confuse these two words. Often the questioner feels that, for all practicable purposes, the refusal of his request will make a barrier over which he *cannot* go. When he says "Can I go," he is feeling, "Will you make it possible for me to go? for unless you consent I cannot go — I cannot afford to, or I cannot conscientiously, or I cannot and remain on right terms with you." Nevertheless, *may* is the only right word to use in asking permission.

Proved, proven.

1. The point was not *proved.*
2. Verdict: "Not proven." *Proven* is a Scotch legal term, wrongly supposed by some persons to be preferable to *proved* out of the court-room.

Purpose, propose.

1. One can't *propose* unless .he proposes something to somebody.

2. One can *purpose* to do a thing, without *proposing* it to any one.

How do both these words contain the idea of *placing?*

Sit, set.

The chief errors in the use of *sit* and *set* are two. Some people insist on saying "*setting hen*" for "*sitting hen,*" and "the coat *sets* well" for "*sits* well." A few say, "*Sit* yourself down," for the somewhat old-fashioned "*sit* you down" (where the *you* is nominative) or for "*set* yourself down." Similarly this error has been known to occur — "he sat the basket of eggs down."

Stay, stop.

1. He *stopped* at Albany; he went no farther.
2. At what hotel are you *staying,* these days?

Transpire, happen.

A good many things *happened* that dark night when the boys were out for a lark; but it never *transpired* what really did happen; nothing leaked out or got to the light.

Spiro means "to breathe" *Trans* (across) when in composition means through, out. Is it not clear how the present use of the word comes about? Explain. Compare the words *expire, conspire, inspire.* How does each get its present meaning?

Wish, want, desire.

1. It is sometimes correct enough to say *want* in the place of *wish*.

2. You shall *want* nothing; all shall be supplied.

3. You shall not want anything you may *desire*.

Which idea springs out of the other — *want* from *wish,* or *wish* from *want?*

ADJECTIVES AND ADVERBS

Apt, likely, liable.

1. He is *apt* at languages.

2. He is *likely* to fail if he does not properly prepare himself. [Here *apt* was possible, but not so good as *likely.*]

Apt means "fitted," "fit." How could such an idea as "It is *apt* to rain this month" spring from the idea of *fit?*

3. He is *likely* to succeed if only he tries.

4. He is *liable* to arrest and quarantine, — though not *likely* to be arrested, — merely because he is *liable* to come down with a contagious disease.

With what kind of feeling does a person look forward to a thing to which he is *liable?*

Continual, continuous.

1. A *continual* dropping is a Biblical phrase.

2. A *continuous* dropping would not be a dropping at all. It would be a stream.

What idea have these words in common?

Funny, odd.

1. It is *odd* that I haven't heard of this before.

2. It is a *funny* sight to see Fido trying desperately to catch his own tail.

Can you explain something of the mental process by which a child comes to say *funny* so frequently, and *strange* so rarely? Is it all a matter of imitation, or is there some other reason? Are there not more of *strange* things in a child's experience than of *funny* things?

Healthy, healthful.

Healthful food makes a *healthy* man.

Give a synonym for *healthful* as applied to food.

Imminent, eminent, immanent.

1. The *eminent* Latin writer, Livy, speaks of Hannibal's elephants as looming up — *eminentes* — through the mist.

2. That God is *immanent* in all the world was a doctrine of the Greek fathers; they meant that he pervades and is diffused throughout it.

3. The sword of Damocles hung *imminent,* suspended by a hair.

4. He is in *imminent* danger of disgrace.

With which two of these words is the idea of *threaten* connected? Which has the idea of *remain,* or *stay,* in it?

In, into.

1. Bruno looked up *into* his master's face.

2. He got *into* the chariot.

3. He sprang *into* the lake, while I stayed *in* the boat.

4. Once *in* the lake, he swam round.

What difference in the use of these words?

Last, latest.

1. The *last* page of the book is done.

2. The *latest* news from the patient is bad.

Does *latest* imply anything as to the future?

Last, preceding.

1. Let each paragraph be joined smoothly with the *preceding*.

2. The *last* paragraph ends the theme.

Mad, angry.

1. There is no reason for being *angry*.

2. Much learning hath made thee *mad*.

3. He was *mad* with rage — fairly insane.

Most, almost.

1. *Most* men are optimists.

2. *Almost* every man loves praise.

Parse the words italicized above.

Mutual, common.

1. Our *common* friend is the better expression, though Dickens has made famous the corresponding worse usage.

2. Friendship may be *mutual;* a friend cannot.

3. Separated by mountains and by *mutual* fear.

What is meant by reciprocal? Which word is a synonym of reciprocal?

Oral, verbal.

1. Miles Standish's act of sending the Indians a snake-skin filled with powder and ball, was a message, but not a *verbal* message.

2. If you are to see John, let me send him this *oral* message: Never say die.

3. The corrections did not affect the truth of the statements, but only the manner: they were *verbal* corrections.

4. The telegraph operator translates into *verbal* form the message that he hears in the ticking of his receiver.

The Latin word *os* means mouth; the Latin word *verbum* means a word. Do *oral* and *verbal* keep the sense of the Latin words? Can a verbal message be oral? Can an oral message be verbal? Is an oral message ordinarily verbal? Can you imagine an oral message that is not verbal?

Posted, informed.

1. The ledger is well *posted.*

2. The editor is well *informed.*

Can you see the slightest reasonable advantage in speaking of a person as well *posted?* In other words, does this commercial slang lend any real force?

Practicable, practical.

His scheme won't work; it isn't *practicable.* I'm afraid he isn't so *practical* a schemer as we thought.

Quite, somewhat, very, rather, entirely, wholly.

1. *Quite* never means " very," " rather," or "somewhat." It means "wholly."
2. Harry is *quite* well; he is never sick.
3. Yes, I like him *rather* well.
4. Thank you; I'm *quite* myself again.

Curtail *quite,* and you get another good English adjective from the same root. How is this shorter word related in sense to the longer? With which of the following expressions can *quite* be used? Well (adj.), sick, recovered, pretty, finished, settled, nice, good, assured, patient, used up, satisfied, a good deal, fine, a hero, a way, a mile, a noise, a failure, a lot, a hundred, a few, a good many, a million, a dozen, some, well (adv.), a while, an hour, your debtor, every one, all, around, through, under, o'erthrown, down, elated, in a rage, underestimate, vanquished, quarrelsome, lovely, everywhere, crestfallen.

Real, really, extremely.

1. I think he's a *real* Count.
2. I think he's *extremely* mean.
3. He's *really* a very fine fellow.

Parse the words italicized above.

Some, somewhat.

1. The sick man is *somewhat* better this morning.
2. *Some* men have greatness thrust upon them.

Parse the words italicized above.

Without, unless.

1. I can't go *unless* there is a holiday.
2. I can't go *without* getting permission.

Parse the words italicized above.

Oral Exercise. — The following sentences are from John Ruskin. No improprieties occur in the originals. Within each pair of brackets a word is given, sometimes the right word, sometimes the wrong word. Study the meaning of each sentence, and satisfy yourself as to what is the best expression for each place in question.

1. The ennobling difference between one man and another — between one animal and another — is precisely in this, that one feels more than another. If we were sponges, perhaps sensation might not be easily [gotten] for us; if we were earth-worms, [apt] at every instant to be cut in two by the spade, perhaps too much sensation might not be good for us.

2. But chiefly of all, she is taught to extend the [limitations] of her sympathy.

3. Very ready we are to say of a book "How good this is — that's exactly what I think!" But

the right feeling is, "How [odd] that is! I never thought of that before, and yet I see it is true; or if I do not now, I hope I shall some day."

4. I believe, then, with this exception, that a girl's education should be nearly, in its course and material of study, the same as a boy's; but [entirely] differently directed. A woman in any rank of life ought to know whatever her husband is [liable] to know, but to know it in a different way.

5. I do not blame them for this, but only for their narrow motive in this. I would have them [want] and [assert] the title of "lady" provided they [allege] not merely the title, but the office and duty signified by it.

6. And not less wrong — perhaps even more foolishly wrong (for I will [expect] thus far what I hope to prove) — is the idea that woman is only the shadow and attendant image of her lord.

7. But now, having no true [avocation], we pour our whole masculine energy into the false business of money-making.

8. Having then faithfully listened to the great teachers, that you may enter into their thoughts, you have yet this higher [advancement] to make, — you have to enter into their hearts.

9. And, lastly, a great nation does not mock Heaven and its Powers by pretending belief in a revelation which [asserts] the love of money to be the root of *all* evil, and [claiming], at the

same time that it is actuated, and [proposes] to be actuated, in all chief national deeds and measures, by no other love.

10. But an education "which shall keep a good coat on my son's back; which shall [capacitate] him to ring with confidence the visitors' bell at double-belled doors; which shall result ultimately in the establishment of a double-belled door to his own [residence] — in a word, which shall lead to [advance] in life — *this* we pray for on bent knees; and this is *all* we pray for." It never seems to occur to the parents that there may be an education which in itself *is* [advance] in Life · that any other than that may perhaps be [advancement] in Death; and that this essential education might be more easily [gotten] or given, than they [guess], if they set about it in the right way, while it is for no price and by no favor to be [got], if they set about it in the wrong.

11. The chance and scattered evil that may here and there haunt, or hide itself in, a powerful book, never does any harm to a noble girl; but the emptiness of an author oppresses her, and his amiable folly [degrades] her. And if she can have [access] to a good library of old and classical books, there need be no choosing at all. Keep the modern magazine and novel out of your girl's way; turn her loose into the old library every day, and [let] her alone.

Oral Exercise. — Examine the italicized words in the following sentences, taken from a newspaper. According to a good dictionary, which are barbarisms? What ones are here incorrectly used? Which ones are colloquial — permitted in talking familiarly, but not in writing? Suggest better expressions.

1. Her prospects for a long career on this earth are *quite* favorable.

2. The galvanic battery was applied every hour without producing any more satisfactory results, but hope did not abandon the *resurrectionists*.

3. When the police arrived they discovered that Burdick was wearing a *bogus* police star and he was arrested.

4. "If you'll throw that gun away and put up your *dukes* like a gentleman, I'll come down there and sew a button *onto* you!"

5. Mr. Hanna was decidedly late in *showing up* at headquarters.

6. It buttons down the front with the finest white pearl buttons of *quite* large size.

7. Makers of sporting goods say there are *a lot* of bicyclists who are ready and waiting to take up every new thing.

8. I *spotted* two of my countrywomen at once.

9. It has been thus far an *exceptionably* busy campaign.

Oral Exercise. — The following sentences are from Stevenson's volume, *Virginibus Puerisque*. As in the preceding exercise, decide on the best word for each place in question.

1. Think of the heroism of Johnson, think of that superb indifference to mortal [limit] that set him upon his dictionary, and carried him through triumphantly to the end!

2. [Most] everybody in our land . . . can understand and sympathize with an admiral or a prize-fighter.

3. When he comes to ride with the king's pardon, he must bestride a chair, which he will so hurry and belabor and on which he will so furiously [demean] himself, that the messenger will arrive, if not bloody with spurring, at least fiery red with haste. If his romance involves an accident upon a cliff, he must clamber in person about the chest of drawers and fall bodily [onto] the carpet, before his imagination is satisfied.

4. Surely all these are [practicable] questions to a neophyte entering upon life with a view to play.

5. A sedentary population . . . can [noways, in no wise] explain to itself the gaiety of these passers-by.

6. To borrow and [demean] an image, all the evening street-lamps burst into song.

7. But the conservative, while lauding progress, is ever timid of innovation; his is the hand upheld

to [council] pause; his is the signal advising slow [advance].

Oral Exercise. — The following sentences are from Mrs. Gaskell's *Cranford*. As before, decide on the best word for each place in question.

1. There were rules and regulations for visiting and calls; and they were announced to any young people, who might be [stopping] in the town.

2. He must have been upwards of sixty at the time of the first visit I paid to Cranford after I had left it as a [residence].

3. She was evidently nervous from having [expected] my call.

4. My request evidently pleased the old gentleman, who took me all [round, around¹] the place, and showed me his six and twenty cows, named after the different letters of the alphabet.

5. I can't [wholly] remember the date, but I think it was in 1805 that Miss Jenkyns wrote the longest [series, succession] of letters.

6. She never laughed at his jokes . . . ; and that [aggravated] him.

7. He was very, very [mad] indeed, and before all the people he lifted up his cane and flogged Peter!

8. "Shell-fish are sometimes thought not very [healthy]."

¹ *Round* is more frequently used than *around* with verbs of motion.

9. The writer of the letter   was dead long ago; and I, a stranger, not born at the time when this occurrence [took place], was the one to open it.

10. I seized the opportunity, and wrote and despatched an [acceptation] in her name.

11. He thought each shawl more beautiful than the [last].

12. I could not see that the little event in the shop below had in the least damped Miss Matty's curiosity as to the make of sleeves or the [set, sit] of skirts. [If neither *sit* nor *set* is right here, how recast the sentence?]

13. Miss Matty [anticipated] the sight of the glossy folds.

14. The Gordons . . . were now [expected] to return very soon; and Miss Matty, in her sisterly pride, [expected] great delight in the joy of showing them Mr. Peter.

15. However, we all sat eyes right, square front, gazing at the [tantalizing] curtain.

16. We (at least I) had doubts as to whether she really would enjoy the little adventure of having her house [burglarized], as she [protested] she would.

17. Miss Jenkyns . . . never got over what she called Captain Brown's disparaging [observations] upon Dr. Johnson as a writer of light and agreeable fiction.

18. It (Death) was a word not to be [alluded to] to ears polite.

Oral Exercise. — The following sentences are from Lord Chesterfield's letters to his son. As in the preceding exercise, choose the best word for each place in question.

1. Your own [remarks] upon mankind, when compared with those which you will find in books, will help you fix the true point.

2. There is nothing which I more wish that you should know, and which [less] people do know, than the true use and value of time.

3. Your [neglect] of dress, while you were a schoolboy, was pardonable, but would not be so now.

4. The [reputations] of kings and great men are only to be learned in conversation; for they are never fairly written during their lives.

5. What does Chesterfield mean by "in a good sense," in the following? "Another, speaking in defence of a gentleman upon whom a censure was moved, happily said that he thought the gentleman was more *liable* to be thanked and rewarded, than censured. You know, I presume, that *liable* can never be used in a good sense."

Review Exercise. — Let each word of the following list be taken up by itself. Each member of the class should give a sentence of his own, using the given word correctly.

Access, acceptance, alternative, avocation, observation, ability, capacity, character, discovery, limitation, party, portion, predominance, residence, except (verb), affect, effect, allude, claim, purpose, transpire, liable, apt, somewhat, quite, mad, practicable.

CHAPTER IX

SOURCES OF THE ENGLISH VOCABULARY

The English Vocabulary. — The enormous treasure of English speech contains something like 200,-000 words.[1] Most of these were once foreigners to the language. To tell how each came to be English would be like telling the personal romances of all the foreign-born citizens of these United States.

England was once inhabited by Celts, the ancestors of the Scotch, Welsh, and Irish. The Romans under Cæsar possessed the island, and for five hundred years held the country, but they left us, from this period of their occupation, only half a dozen words: the names of the camp (*castra*), the paved road (*strata*), the settlement (*colonia*), the trench (*fossa*), the harbor (*portus*), the rampart (*vallum*). These words remain chiefly in the names of places. A sharp eye sees them in Lancaster,

[1] Probably three-fourths of these words are not in literary use to-day. Many are obsolete, many are colloquial, many are scientific or technical. Thousands of other scientific terms (names of genera and species) are not included in the 200,000 estimate.

Leicester, Manchester, etc.; Stratford, street, etc.; Lincoln, etc.; Fossway, etc.; Portsmouth, etc.; wall, bailey, bailiff (these three words being derived from *vallum*).

In the fifth century, however, Teutonic tribes began to cross the sea and invade the land. The Celts were driven north and west into the mountains, and the newcomers stayed permanently. Although these Teutons — the Anglo-Saxons — called the Celts *Welsh*, that is, strangers, they took up a good many of the strangers' words. They called many a river of the land *Avon*, water, as the Celts had done, — there are fourteen Avons to-day, — and they kept many such words as *inch*, an island (in Inchcape), and *kill*, a church (in Kildare). Indeed, for centuries the Celts kept on lending words to the English: *bargain, bodkin, brogue, clan, crag, dagger, glen, gown, mitten, rogue, whiskey,* are familiar examples of these permanent loans.

The Old English language itself was a Germanic dialect. Like Latin and German, it was inflected, — a fact that we see to-day in the presence of such forms as *him*, the old dative case for *he*. The inflectional endings nearly all disappeared before Shakespeare's time. The vocabulary of this Old English has given us most of the words that we use as children. For example, household names — *home, friends, father, mother,* etc.; names of many emotions — *gladness, sorrow, love, hate, fear,* etc.;

names of most objects in the landscape — *tree, bush, stone, hill, woods, stream, sun, moon,* etc.; common names of animals — *horse, cow, dog, cat,* etc.; parts of the body — *head, eye,* etc. Our household proverbs are in these Anglo-Saxon words. "Fast bind, fast find," is an example of a thousand similar saws that embody the practical common sense of the people. The loves and hates, the hopes and fears, the wit and rude wisdom of our forefathers, have gone into Saxon words. These are not merely the words of childhood; in hours of deep feeling, in moments when the natural disposition demands expression, the grown man speaks in Saxon. These strong, forcible old words are to be prized and cherished as carefully as are those of less emotional suggestion, — the exact, discriminative Latin words.

In the ninth and tenth centuries the Norse vikings, who sailed everywhere, sailed also to England, and for a time got the upper hand of the Saxons. From 1013 to 1042 there were Scandinavian kings on the English throne. But these Norse were not able to impose much of their own language upon the country. Their settlements were named in Norse, and the word *by,* a town, remains in hundreds of such places, as *Whitby,* the *white town* (from the white cliffs). From these great seamen our Saxon ancestors learned some new nautical dialect — words like *bow, bowline, crew, harbor, hawser, lee, stern.*

In 1066 the Normans conquered the land. These were Frenchmen whose fathers had been Norse. They brought the French language into their English court, and for two or three hundred years there were two languages in England, — French on the lips of the nobles, Saxon on the lips of the peasants. But the Saxon race was too strong to remain an underling. Gradually it mingled with the Norman race, picking up hundreds, even thousands of French words from the latter, but keeping its own ways of putting words together.

By 1400, when Chaucer died, there was a new English language, almost as much French as Saxon in vocabulary, but far less French than Saxon in grammar. Since French is largely derived from Latin, it is clear that the total Latin element in the vocabulary was already very great.

After Chaucer there came a general awakening of interest in ancient civilization; and in the Revival of Learning a great many words were adopted directly from Latin and Greek. In the sixteenth century followed the Renaissance of literature, art, and the sciences. This made its way to England from Italy, and naturally Englishmen caught up many new words from Italians. For example: *alert, bankrupt, brigade, bust, cameo, caricature, cascade, domino, fresco, granite, influenza, malaria, niche, oratorio, pianoforte, ruffian, studio, tirade, umbrella, vista.* The Spaniards, too, whom

Englishmen met in those days on the sea and at courts, have lent our language such words as *barricade, bravado, cigar, desperado, flotilla, guerilla, merino, mosquito, mulatto, renegade, sherry, tornado, vanilla.*

The bold English seamen of the sixteenth century sailed back even from America with new things and new names — like *tobacco.* In the next century the commerce which followed hard upon the voyages of discovery was the means of bringing to the British island many new words. Here it may be said that the Dutch, who have rivalled the English in commerce, and who have taught the English some tricks of seamanship, — as did the vikings before them, — are represented in English by words like *ballast, boom, boor, skipper, sloop, smack, trigger, yacht.* English merchantmen of the seventeenth and eighteenth centuries sailed to ports Oriental and Occidental. Returning, they brought from Africa canaries and gorillas, with the words *canary* and *gorilla,* and told of *oases;* from Arabia they fetched such names as *admiral, alcohol, alcove, alkali, arsenal, azure, chemistry, coffee, cotton, lute, magazine, nabob, naphtha, sherbet, sofa, syrup, zenith;* indeed, some of these words had got into English through earlier English travellers — chiefly crusaders. English sailors and travellers have brought from China *silk, tea,* etc.; from India, *banyan, calico, mullagatawny, musk, punch, sugar, thug,* etc.; from Malayan ports, *bantam, cockatoo, gong, rattan, sugo,* etc.; from Persia, *awning, caravan, chess, hazard, horde, lemon, orange, paradise, sash, shawl,* etc. Few are the languages from which a British ear has not caught and kept a new term.

In America we have many Indian names of places and things. We have *hominy, moose, opossum, raccoon, toboggan,* and other words from North American tribes. Mexico gave us *chocolate, tomato,* etc.; the West Indies, *potato, canoe, hurricane;* South America, *alpaca, quinine, tapioca,* etc.

In the present century, science, both practical and pure, has discovered thousands of facts and invented thousands of contrivances. Consequently thousands of words have been coined, mostly from Greek, to name modern inventions and the facts of science. A recent dictionary found it necessary to codify 4000 technical terms that had sprung up within the last few years.

Anglo-Saxon Prefixes and Suffixes. — The following prefixes are Anglo-Saxon. Think of words made with each.

1. *A-* = in, on.
2. *Be-.* What grammatical effect has this prefix on *moan, daub, friend* ?
3. *For-.* What effect has this on *bid, lorn* ? Compare Latin *per,* in *perfect.*
4. *Fore-.*   5. *Gain-* = against.
6. *Mis-* (A.-S. *mis* = wrong). What effect on *deed,*

lead? A French prefix from Latin *minus* occurs in *mis-chief*, etc.

    7. *Th-.*   8. *Un-.*
    9. *With-* (A.-S. *wither* = back).

Similarly think of words made with each of the following *noun* suffixes and explain the force of each suffix.

    1. *-ard* = habitual.   2. *-craft.*
    3. *-dom.*   4. *-en.*
    5. *-er.*   6. *-hood.*

    7. *-ing* = son of, part. Meaning of *Browning?* *lording?* *tithing?* There is an older suffix which appears in the gerund — *taking, hunting.*

    8. *-kin.*   9. *-ling.*
    10. *-ness.*   11. *-ock.*
    12. *-ric* = power.   13. *-ship.*
    14. *-stead* = place.   15. *-ster.*
    16. *-wright.*   17. *-ward.*

Think of words made with the following *adjective* suffixes.

    1. *-ed.*   2. *-en.*
    3. *-ern.*   4. *-fast.*
    5. *-fold.*   6. *-ful.*
    7. *-ish.*   8. *-less.*
    9. *-like* (*lic* = body, form).   10. *-right.*
    11. *-some* = same.   12. *-y.*

Think of words made with the following *adverb* suffixes.

    1. *-es* (the old genitive ending).
    2. *-ly* (*lic* = body, form).   3. *-ling, -long.*
    4. *-meal.*   5. *-om* (old dative plural).
    6. *-ward.*   7. *-wise* = manner.

The Latin Element. — The Latin element is numerically the larger part of the language. It is therefore impossible to know well the English vocabulary except by knowing a considerable part of the Latin language. Whether our Latin words come directly through the ancient classics, or through the Romance tongues, such as French, Italian, and Spanish, to know their full force one must know the original meaning of them, as used by the ancient race of world-conquerors. Every instructor in English watches with keen interest the progress made by his students in their Latin studies. Of course, the mere knowledge that a given word is derived from a given Latin word does not necessarily give the student practical command of it in his writing; but usually such knowledge does help to a better understanding of the meaning the word has to-day, and so tends both to fix it in memory and to insure exact use of it.

Latin Words transferred to English. — Some Latin words have been transferred bodily into English. Discuss with the instructor the derivation of the present meanings of the following : —

Alias = otherwise ; *album* = white ; *amanuensis* = hand-writer ; *animus* = mind; *arena* = sand; *boa* = great serpent; *camera* = chamber; *cornucopia* = horn of plenty; *extra* = beyond ; *focus* = hearth ; *gratis* = for nothing ; *item* = also; *memento* = remember (imperative) ; *nostrum* = our own ;

omnibus = for all ; *posse* = to be able ; *quorum* = of whom ; *rebus* = by things ; *rostrum* = beak ; *torpedo* = numbness ; *vagary* = to wander ; *videlicet* = it can be seen ; *virago* = a mannish woman.

Latin Prefixes and Suffixes. — Recall English words having the following prefixes, and explain the effect of the prefix on each.

A-, *ab-*, *abs-* = from ; *ad-* = to ; *amb-* = about ; *ante-* = before ; *bis-*, *bi-* = twice ; *circum-* = around ; *cum-* (found in French *col-*, *com-*, cor-, *coun-*) = with ; *contra-* = against ; *de-* = down, from ; *dis-* (Fr. *des-*, *de-*) = asunder ; *ex-* (Fr. *es-*, *e-*) = from ; *extra-* = beyond ; *in-* (Fr. *en-*, *em-*) = in, into ; *in-* (*il-*, *im-*, *ir-*, *ig-*) = not ; *inter-* = between, among ; *non-* = not ; *ob-* = against ; *pene-* = almost ; *per-* = through ; *post-* = after ; *præ-*, *pre-* = before ; *præter-* = beyond ; *pro-* (Fr. *pour* = *pol-*, *por-*, *pur-*) = for ; *re-* = back ; *retro-* = backwards ; *se-* = apart ; *sub-* (*suc-*, *suf-*, *sum-*, *sup-*, *sur-*, *sus-*) = under ; *super-* = above ; *trans-* = across ; *vice-* = in place of.

Recall words having the following Latin or Latin-French suffixes, and explain each in terms of the meaning of the suffix.

-Aceous (Lat. *-aceus*) = made of ; *-al* (Latin *-alis*) = pertaining to ; *-able* (*-ible*), Lat. *(h)abilis* = capable of being ; *-ple*, *-ble* (Latin *-plex*) = fold ; *-plex* = fold ; *-lent* (Lat. *-lentus*) = full of ; *-ose* (Lat. *-osus*) = full of ; *-und* (Lat. *-undus*) = full of ; *-ulous* (Lat. *-ulus*) = full of.

Latin Roots in English. — Below are listed a few of the many Latin words that have given us English words. Recall as many as possible of their derivatives, and define each in terms of the original

meaning. Thus *acer,* sharp, gives us *acrimony,*
sharpness, *acrid,* sour. Some member of the class
may know that through the French it gives us
vinegar, sharp wine. Make notes in your note-book
of any derivatives that are new to you. *Ædes,* a
building; *æquus,* equal; *ager,* a field; *agere,* to do;
alere, to nourish — perfect participle *altus,* nour-
ished, therefore high; *amare,* to love; *anima,* life;
animus, mind; *annus,* a year; *aqua,* water; *arcus,*
a bow; *ardere* (pf. ptc. *arsus*), to burn; *audire,* to
hear; *augere* (pf. ptc. *auctus*), to increase; *brevis,*
brief; *cadere* (pf. ptc. *casus*), to fall; *candere,* to
shine; *capere,* to take; *caput,* a head; *cavus,* hollow;
cernere (pf. ptc. *cretus*), to distinguish; *clarus,* clear;
cor, heart; *corona,* crown; *credere,* to believe; *cre-
scere* (pf. ptc. *cretus*), to grow; *crudus,* raw; *cura,*
care; *deus,* god; *dicere,* to say; *docere,* to teach;
dominus, lord (Fr. *damsel, dame, madame*); *domus,*
a house; *ducere,* to lead; *errare,* to wander; *facere,*
to make; *filum,* a thread; *finis,* the end; *flos,* a
flower; *frangere* (stems, *frag, fract*), to break;
fortis, strong; *fundere,* to pour; *gradus,* a step;
gravis, heavy; *homo,* a man; *imperare,* to command; *jus,* right; *legere* (*lect*), to read; *ligo,* to bind;
litera, a letter; *loqui,* to speak; *lumen,* light; *luna,*
the moon; *magnus,* great; *manus,* a hand; *matu-
rus,* ripe; *mittere* (*missere*), to send; *mors,* death;
novus, new; *nox,* night; *omnis,* all; *ordo,* order;
pascere (pf. ptc. *pastus*), to feed; *pati* (pf. ptc.

passus), to suffer; *petere*, to seek; *portare*, to carry; *radix*, a root; *regere* (pf. ptc. *rectus*), to rule; *scire*, to know; *sequi* (pf. ptc. *secutus*), to follow; *socius*, a companion; *spirare*, to breathe; *tangere*, to touch; *texere*, to weave; *vanus*, empty; *videre*, to see· *vincere* (pf. ptc. *victus*), to conquer; *vulgus*, the crowd.

Greek Roots in English. — Recall English words made from the following Greek roots, and explain each. Make notes in your note-book of those derivatives that are new to you. *Anthropos*, a man; *aster*, *astron*, a star; *autos*, self; *biblos*, a book; *bios*, life; *deka*, ten; *dokein*, to think; *dunamis*, power; *eu*, well; *ge*, the earth; *graphein*, to write; *hemi*, half; *hippos*, a horse; *homos*, the same; *kuklos*, a circle; *monos*, alone; *orthos*, right; *pan*, all; *petra*, a rock; *philein*, to love; *phone*, a sound; *poiein*, to make; [1] *skopein*, to see; *sophia*, wisdom· *tele*, distant; *theos*, a god.

Curious Words. — Look up and copy into your note-book the origin of the following words. *Assassin, august, dahlia, dunce, epicure, galvanic, guillotine, hermetically, January, jovial, July, lynch, March, mentor, panic, phaeton, quixotic, stentorian, tantalize, tawdry. Bayonet, bedlam, copper, damask, dollar, gasconade, gipsy, laconic, lumber, meander,*

---

[1] A maker of noble verse is called what ?

milliner, palace, utopian. Abominate, adieu, amethyst, apothecary, beldam, capricious, cemetery, cheap, checkmate, cobalt, curmudgeon, dainty, daisy, dismal, emolument, salary, fanatic, gentleman, heretic, inculcate, infant, intoxicated, maidenhair (fern), *maxim, nausea, onyx, parlor, Porte* (the Sublime Porte) *pupil, silly, sincere, tariff, trump* (card). *Atonement, belfry, brimstone, carouse, counterpane, coward, crayfish, dandelion, dirge, drawing-room, easel, gospelgrove, harbinger, Jerusalem artichoke, line* (garments), *licorice, nostril, porpoise, quinsy, squirrel, summerset, surgeon, thorough, treacle, trifle, wassail, whole.*

Written Exercise. — Examine the following passages separately. Classify all the words in two columns, one giving those of Saxon derivation, the other those of Latin derivation. Consult the dictionary in case of doubt. Then compare the English of Dr. Johnson with that of Dr. Blackmore. The former is writing in his own person as an eighteenth century scholar; the latter in the person of the stout John Ridd, a seventeenth century youth.

No degree of knowledge attainable by man is able to set him above the want of hourly assistance, or to extinguish the desire of fond endearments, and tender officiousness; and therefore, no one should think it unnecessary to learn those arts by which friendship may be gained. Kindness is preserved by a constant reciprocation of benefits or interchange of pleasures ; but such benefits only can be bestowed as others are capable to receive, and such pleasures only imparted, as others are qualified to enjoy. — DR. JOHNSON, *Rambler for July 9, 1751.*

When *I* had travelled two miles or so, conquered now and then with cold, and coming out to rub my legs into a lively friction, and only fishing here and there because of the tumbling water, suddenly, in an open space, where meadows spread about it, *I* found a good stream flowing softly into the body of our brook. And it brought, so far as *I* could guess by the sweep of it under my knee-caps, a larger power of clear water than the Lynn itself had ; only it came more quietly down, not being troubled with stairs and steps, as the fortune of the Lynn is, but gliding smoothly and forcibly, as if upon some set purpose. — R. D. BLACKMORE, *Lorna Doone.*

CHAPTER X

THE MASTERY OF A WRITING VOCABULARY

Ideas without Words. — It is possible to have ideas without having words in which to express them. Miss Helen Keller[1] had plenty of ideas before any one taught her the words for them. The painter trains himself to express ideas in paint; the sculptor, in stone. The inventor expresses ideas in machinery. Because words however are the commonest means of expression, it is desirable that one should know as many as possible. A person who has ideas will indeed be able to communicate them in some rough-and-ready form of speech; will use a poor word, if he cannot think of a good one, and by hook or crook will manage to be understood. But an unread, untrained man trying to communicate some fine shade of thought is commonly a sorry sight, no matter how bright his mind may be.

Words without Ideas. — On the other hand, it is possible to know words without knowing what they

[1] See *The Century Magazine* for November, 1896, for an English theme by Miss Helen.

stand for. Some persons of quick verbal memory pick up phrases readily, and utter them glibly, with little sense of their meaning. Gratiano, of Shakespeare's drama, "spoke an infinite deal of nothing, more than any man in Venice." Such persons as he have given ground for the sarcastic remark that language is the art of concealing thought. The use of meaningless phrases, and the use of words without a care to their exact meaning, is one danger that besets the student of composition. The boy who fluently remarks that he recently lost his little *saturnine* (meaning *canine*, i.e. *dog*); the lady, Mrs. Malaprop, who walks through Sheridan's play, saying, "You go first, and we'll *precede* you"; the man, Launcelot Gobbo, who enlivens *The Merchant of Venice* with such remarks as that "his suit is *impertinent* to himself," — these people need a book of synonyms. Unless a writer is sure that he knows definitely the meaning of the word that his pen is about to trace, he would much better stay his hand.

Ideas and Words. — Though one mind may have ideas but lack their names, and though another may have the names but lack the notions for which they stand, yet both ideas and words are indispensable to the writer. A general recipe for getting ideas is hardly easier to give than a recipe for being great, or for having blue eyes, or for being liked by every one. Ideas are had through new experiences, new acquaintanceships, new sights; through hard thinking, through hard reading,—in short, through living. Mr. Henry James, the eminent novelist, gives a direction for being a good novelist: *Try to be one of those people on whom nothing is lost.* The student who is eager to know as much as possible of what is worth knowing in life, and is devoured with curiosity to learn the name of everything, is sure to acquire both new ideas and new words.[1]

It is nevertheless not to be denied that to some extent ideas can be bred by the study of the mere words. How true this is appears when it is remembered that words are the embalmed ideas of men. A study of such a list as the Curious Words given in the preceding chapter cannot but add to the student's mental stores. Thackeray, it is said, used to read the dictionary before he composed. It may be presumed that the habit used not merely to acquaint him with new words, but to arouse his mind and set it to fashioning new thoughts. The attempt to discriminate between words that mean nearly, not quite, the same thing, results in a distinct gain in thought, and in power of thought. It is probable that no two words have exactly the same sense; to discover the difference enriches the

[1] Emerson's words, quoted on page 121, will occur to every reader.

discoverer's store of knowledge, and develops one of the highest mental powers. A command of words not merely affords relief from the pain of dumbness, not merely loosens the tongue; it aids reasoning. Thinking proceeds more securely the moment a hazy notion is given definite shape in the right word. Indeed, the mere search for the right word is always a means of clearing up the thought. To be tortured in mind by inability to find the unique phrase, sometimes means a mere fault in verbal memory; as often, or oftener, it is due to a vagueness of thinking.

By way of summary, then, acquisition of ideas furthers acquisition of words, and *vice versâ*. To be poor in ideas, or to be poor in language, — either means failure for a writer.

The Two Vocabularies. — Of all the 200,000 words in our language, probably no one man would understand one-half if he saw them, undefined, in a dictionary. Just how large a man's reading vocabulary can be is not known. Professor Holden, the astronomer, found that his own was about 33,000 words. It is therefore likely that 25,000 is not an unusual number for an educated person to understand. But the *reading* or *passive* vocabulary is very different in size from the *writing* or *active* vocabulary. To remember the sense of a word when it is seen is far less difficult than to re-

call the word whenever its meaning rises dimly in
the mind. A little child has but one set of words
— an active vocabulary; it makes oral use of all the
expressions it knows. But the older person reads so
much that he comes to recognize myriads of words
that rarely rise to his lips or find their way to his
pen. There is inevitably therefore a widening gap
between the expressions he can recognize and those
he can employ. That this should be so is in part desirable. A person of fourteen or sixteen or eighteen must, if he reads carefully, learn to understand
many expressions that are too bookish for his own
uses. The word *temerarious*, for instance, is needed
once where its unpretentious cousin, *rash*, is needed
a score of times. With some words the young
writer needs only a speaking acquaintance; others
are good friends that, in Hamlet's phrase, he should
buckle to his soul with hoops of steel. But it is
safe to say that if a person can transfer some part
of his reading vocabulary into his writing vocabulary, he will be much benefited by so doing.
There is probably no reason why a freshman should
not enter college master of a writing vocabulary
of 5000 words, and a reading vocabulary of 15,000.
Shakespeare's works contain about 15,000 different
words, the King James version of the Bible fewer
than 6000. Again, each person uses the same
words with many different meanings. Every great
writer employs the same words in many figurative

senses; the fact is perhaps the most striking proof of his literary power. If Shakespeare's vocabulary were reckoned as including these figurative meanings, it would shoot up to a wonderful figure.

"It would be absurd," says Professor A. S. Hill, with characteristic good sense, "for a boy to have the desirableness of enlarging his vocabulary constantly on his mind; but if he avails himself of his opportunities, in the school-room or out of it, he will be surprised to find how rapidly his vocabulary grows." Doubtless however the matter must receive some definite attention, if the best results are to be secured. In the rest of this chapter particular methods of acquiring new words and senses of words will be considered.

A Vocabulary Book. — It will be found helpful to buy a strong blank-book of convenient size, and to copy into this every new word that seems to the student available for his writing; not every new word he meets, for some will impress him as too bookish or pedantic, but those which appear to express happily some idea that has lain unnamed in his mind.

Figurative Uses of Common Words. — A writer owes it to himself and to the reader to get all the service he legitimately can out of common words, because in the end so doing spares both persons a vast deal of unnecessary labor. Examine a handful of the well-worn counters of speech, — such words as *poor, heavy, thin, best, full, manner, sense, deep, sweet.* They are like dull pebbles brought home from the beach. But dip them back into the brine of a good book, and they become gems. The words specified above appear in a paragraph of Mr. W. D. Howells: "I followed Irving, too, in my later reading, but at haphazard, and with other authors at the same time. I did my poor best to be amused by his *Knickerbocker History of New York,* because my father liked it so much, but secretly I found it heavy; and a few years ago when I went carefully through it again, I could not laugh. Even as a boy I found some other things of his up-hill work. There was the beautiful manner, but the thought seemed thin; and I do not remember having been much amused by *Bracebridge Hall,* though I read it devoutly, and with a full sense that it would be very *comme il faut* to like it. But I did like the life of Goldsmith; I liked it a great deal better than the more authoritative life by Forster, and I think there is a deeper and sweeter sense of Goldsmith in it."[1]

Observe the various duties that the plainest words were persuaded into doing for Shakespeare. With him the word *old* applies to widely different things: *Old arms, old beard, old limbs, old eyes, old bones, old feet, old heart, old wrinkles, old wit, old*

[1] *My Literary Passions,* p. 32 (Harper & Bros.).

care, old woe, old hate, old custom, old days. What does each of these phrases mean? He is fond of contrasting simple words; thus, " He'll take his *old* course in a country *new.*"

Note how many abstract ideas in Shakespeare are contented with the word *heavy,* which ordinary people apply merely to coal, lead, and such uninspiring commodities. *Heavy accent, heavy news, heavy sin, heavy act, heavy task, heavy day, heavy hour, heavy gait, heavy leave, heavy message, heavy summons.* Explain what each means.[1]

Similarly there are *light gifts, light behavior, light heart, light loss, light of foot, light wings, light foam.* Another drudge of a word, *thick,* learns new and pleasanter tasks of the great poet. *Thick sight, thick perils, thick in their thoughts, thick sighs, thick slumber.* Explain each of these phrases. Opposed to *thick* is *thin: thin air, thin drink, thin and slender pittance.* These are the things that Shakespeare calls *high: high deeds, high descent, high desert, high designs, high disgrace, high exploits, high feats, high good trim, high heaven, high hope, high perfection, high resolve, high reward.* One more word, *golden.* Lesser poets would apply it to physical objects. Shakespeare, too, speaks of the sun " Kissing with golden face the meadows green," and of " This majestical roof fretted with golden fire " But else-

[1] In case of doubt, consult Bartlett's *Shakspere Concordance* (Macmillan Co.).

where he manages to apply the adjective to things that cannot so directly be called golden. Thus "A golden mind stoops not to shows of dross."

wear a golden sorrow." "Golden lads and girls all must, As chimney sweepers, come to dust." "Nestor's golden words" Explain each of these uses.

Of course many of these figurative expressions are too poetical by far for the prose of high school students. Nevertheless, many others would be appropriate in the manuscript of any person, — for instance, *high designs, high deeds, high exploits, high resolve.* Such uses as these can be cultivated to the enrichment of the vocabulary.

Written Exercise.[1] — Each of the following adjectives applies primarily to physical objects, that can be seen, or heard, or touched, or tasted. But each is often raised to a higher use, being made to name some quality of character, or some other abstract idea. Take the adjectives one by one, and under each write in class as many abstract words as you think can properly be modified by the given adjective. Thus the adjective *fine*, which is used of such physical objects as *sand, cloth, particles,* may also apply to *courage, sense of honor presence, phrases, words, deeds.*

[1] It may be found desirable to assign only a part of the words to each student, the results to be read before the class and discussed.

1. Sweet. 2. Sour. 3. Bitter. 4. Soft. 5. Hard.
6. Smooth. 7. Rough. 8. Delicious. 9. Insipid.
10. Cold. 11. Freezing. 12. Icy. 13. Burning.
14. Chilly. 15. Blue. 16. White. 17. Black.
18. Gray. 19. Brown. 20. Green. 21. Dark.
22. Shadowy. 23. Misty. 24. Cloudy. 25. Windy.
26. Stormy. 27. Transparent. 28. Blunt. 29. Sharp.
30. Keen. 31. Dull. 32. Fragrant. 33. Malodorous. 34. Shining. 35. Beaming. 36. Glowing.
37. Glittering. 38. Blazing. 39. Hazy. 40. Brilliant. 41. Muddy. 42. Rippling.

The Value of Careful Reading. — A writer must perhaps be as dependent on books for his vocabulary as on any other one source. Yet it is possible to read a great deal without absorbing many new expressions. To gain new words and new ideas, the student must compel himself to read slowly. Impatient to hurry on and learn how the tale or poem ends, many a youth is accustomed to read so rapidly as to miss the best part of what the author is trying to say. Thoughts cannot be read so rapidly as words. To get at the thoughts and really to retain the valuable expressions, the student must scrutinize and ponder as he reads. Each word must be thoroughly understood; its exact value in the given sentence must be grasped. It will not do to draft off a long list of new expressions into the note-book, and then investigate the meaning of each after the connection in which each was used has been forgotten. Usually the best way is to look up the meaning when the word is come upon. This is always the best way when a passage is being read with a view to increasing one's vocabulary. When a tale or poem or essay is being read for its general theme, or for its literary construction, it is often desirable to underline each new word, leaving the meaning to be investigated a little later. In finding the value of the word in its sentence, the student is often little aided by the dictionary. Imagination and reasoning must sometimes be called into play before the definition can be made to apply. The dictionary — partienlarly the abridged dictionary — is not a magic book, ready to explain every delicate shading that a great author gives a word in a particular connection.

In reading silently it is due the author to read with as much expression as if one were pronouncing the words aloud. One should mentally give every word and phrase its proper accent, should feel the value of every punctuation mark. The force of such a passage as the following, from Carlyle, will be lost unless the reader puts the emphasis in exactly the right places.

Manhood begins when we have in any way made truce with *N*ecessity ; begins, at all events, when we have surrendered to *N*ecessity, as the most part only do ; but begins joyfully and hopefully only when we have reconciled our-selves to *N*ecessity ; and thus, in reality, triumphed over it, and felt that in *N*ecessity we are free.

Literature is full of words descriptive of things that all have seen or heard. We render a ser-vice to the memory if in reading we linger long enough to call up the colors, shapes, motions, sounds, that are suggested by the text. Some per-sons recall sights more easily than sounds, some recall sounds more easily than sights ; some can remember motions more easily than either colors, shapes, or sounds. It is therefore good training for the word-memory if we endeavor to recall all kinds of sense impressions. Read the following passage slowly, imagining the sights, motions, and sensations of touch, that are suggested.

A long way down that limpid water, chill and bright as an iceberg, went my little self that day on man's choice errand — destruction. All the young fish seemed to know that *I* was one who had taken out God's certificate, and meant to have the value of it ; every one of them was aware that we desolate more than replenish the earth. For a cow might come and look into the water, and put her yellow lips down ; a kingfisher, like a blue arrow, might shoot through the dark alleys over the channel, or sit on a dipping withy-bough with his beak sunk into his breast-feathers ; even an otter might float down stream, likening himself to a log of wood, with his flat head flush with the water-top, and his oily eyes peering quietly ; and yet no panic would seize other life, as it does when a sample of man comes. — R. D. BLACK-MORE, *Lorna Doone.*

Imagine as vividly as possible each sound and other physical sensation suggested by the following selection, from the book just quoted: —

The volumes of the mist came rolling at me (like great logs of wood, pillowed out with sleepiness), and between them there was nothing more than waiting for the next one. Then everything went out of sight, and glad was *I* of the stone behind me, and view of mine own shoes. Then a distant noise went by me, as of many horses galloping, and in my fright *I* set my gun and said, "God send something to shoot at." Yet nothing came, and my gun fell back, without my will to lower it.

But presently, while I was thinking "What a fool *I* am!" arose as if from below my feet, so that the great stone trembled, that long lamenting, lonesome sound, as of an evil spirit not knowing what to do with it. *F*or the moment *I* stood like a root, without either hand or foot to help me, and the hair of my head began to crawl, lifting my hat, as a snail lifts his house, and my heart like a shuttle went to and fro. But finding no harm to come of it, neither visible form approaching, *I* wiped my forehead and hoped for the best, and resolved to run every step of the way till *I* drew our own latch behind me.

Yet here again I was disappointed, for no sooner was *I* come to the cross-ways by the black pool in the hole, but I heard through the patter of my own feet a rough low sound very close in the fog, as of a hobbled sheep a-coughing. *I* listened, and feared, and yet listened again, though *I* wanted not to hear it. For being in haste of the homeward road, and all my heart having heels to it, loath I was to stop in the dusk for the sake of an aged wether. Yet partly my love of all animals, and partly my fear of the farmer's disgrace, compelled me to go to the succor, and the noise was coming nearer. A dry, short, wheezing sound it was, barred with coughs and want of breath; but thus *I* made the meaning of it: —

What do you see mentally, when you read the following ?

> Sweet are the uses of adversity,
> Which, like the toad, ugly and venomous,
> Wears yet a precious jewel in its head.

The value of minute and thoughtful reading has been set forth by John Ruskin, in his *Sesame and Lilies,* a book well worth reading, if one is willing to take in good part the earnest, somewhat dogmatic tone which Ruskin so often uses. The oft-quoted passage in which he illustrates his idea of how a poem should be read, is given below. The student who every day reads a few pages as conscientiously as Ruskin would have him, will find his command of words rapidly increasing, and his power of thought increasing likewise.

And now, merely for example's sake, *I* will, with your permission, read a few lines of a true book with you carefully, and see what will come out of them. *I* will take a book perfectly known to you all. No English words are more familiar to us, yet few perhaps have been read with less sincerity. *I* will take these few following lines of *Lycidas :*

> " Last came, and last did go,
> The pilot of the Galilean lake.
> Two massy keys he bore of metals twain
> (The golden opes, the iron shuts amain) :
> He shook his mitred locks, and stern bespake :
> ' How well could I have spared for thee, young swain,
> Enow of such as for their bellies' sake
> Creep and intrude and climb into the fold !
> Of other care they little reckoning make
> Than how to scramble at the shearers' feast,
> And shove away the worthy bidden guest ;
> Blind mouths! that scarce themselves know how to hold

A sheep-hook, or have learned aught else, the least
That to the faithful herdsman's art belongs!
What recks it them? What need they? They are sped;
And when they list, their lean and flashy songs
Grate on their scrannel pipes of wretched straw.
The hungry sheep look up, and are not fed,
But swoln with wind, and the rank mist they draw,
Rot inwardly, and foul contagion spread,
Besides what the grim wolf with privy paw
Daily devours apace, and nothing said.' "

Let us think over this passage, and examine its words.

First, is it not singular to find Milton assigning to St. Peter, not only his full episcopal function, but the very types of it which Protestants usually refuse most passionately? His "mitred" locks! Milton was no Bishop-lover; how comes St. Peter to be "mitred"? "Two massy keys he bore." Is this, then, the power of the keys claimed by the bishops of Rome, and is it acknowledged here by Milton only in a poetical license, for the sake of its picturesqueness, that he may get the gleam of the golden keys to help his effect? Do not think it. Great men do not play stage tricks with doctrines of life and death: only little men do that. Milton means what he says; and means it with his might too — is going to put the whole strength of his spirit presently into the saying of it. For though not a lover of false bishops, he *was* a lover of true ones; and the Lake-pilot is here, in his thoughts, the type and head of true episcopal power. For Milton reads that text, "*I* will give unto thee the keys of the kingdom of Heaven" quite honestly. Puritan though he be, he would not blot it out of the book because there have been bad bishops; nay, in order to understand him, we must understand that verse first; it will not do to eye it askance, or whisper it under our breath, as if it were a weapon of an adverse sect. *It* is a solemn, universal assertion, deeply to be kept in mind by all sects. But perhaps we shall be better able to reason on it if we go on a little farther, and come back to it. For clearly, this marked insistence on the power of the true episcopate is to make us feel more weightily what is to be charged against the false claimants of episcopate; or generally, against false claimants of power and rank in the body of the clergy; they who, "for their bellies' sake, creep, and intrude, and climb into the fold."

Do not think Milton uses those three words to fill up his verse, as a loose writer would. He needs all the three; specially those three, and no more than those — "creep" and "intrude," and "climb"; no other words would or could serve the turn, and no more could be added. For they exhaustively comprehend the three classes, correspondent to the three characters, of men who dishonestly seek ecclesiastical power. First, those who "creep" into the fold, who do not care for office, nor name, but for secret influence, and do all things occultly and cunningly, consenting to any servility of office or conduct, so only that they may intimately discern, and unawares direct, the minds of men. Then those who "intrude" (thrust, that is) themselves into the fold, who by natural insolence of heart and stout eloquence of tongue and fearlessly perseverant self-assertion obtain hearing and authority with the common crowd. Lastly, those who "climb," who, by labor and learning both stout and sound, but selfishly exerted in the cause of their own ambition, gain high dignities and authorities, and become "lords over the heritage," though not "ensamples to the flock."

Now go on:

> "Of other care they little reckoning make
> Than how to scramble at the shearers' feast.
> *Blind mouths —*"

I pause again, for this is a strange expression, — a broken metaphor, one might think, careless and unscholarly.

Not so; its very audacity and pithiness are intended to make us look close at the phrase and remember it. Those two monosyllables express the precisely accurate contraries of right character, in the two great offices of the Church those of bishop and pastor.

A Bishop means a person who sees.

A Pastor means one who feeds.

The most unbishoply character a man can have is therefore to be Blind.

The most unpastoral is, instead of feeding to want to be fed, — to be a Mouth.

Take the two reverses together, and you have "blind mouths." We may advisably follow out this idea a little. Nearly all the evils in the Church have arisen from bishops desiring *power* more than *light*. They want authority, not outlook. Whereas their real office is not to rule ; though it may be vigorously to exhort and rebuke ; it is the king's office to rule ; the bishop's office is to *oversee* the flock ; to number it, sheep by sheep ; to be ready always to give full account of it. Now it is clear he cannot give account of the souls, if he has not so much as numbered the bodies of his flock. The first thing, therefore, that a bishop has to do is at least to put himself in a position in which, at any moment, he can obtain the history from childhood of every living soul in his diocese, and of its present state. Down in that back street, Bill, and Nancy, knocking each other's teeth out! — Does the bishop know all about it? Has he his eye upon them ? Has he *had* his eye upon them ? Can he circumstantially explain to us how Bill got into the habit of beating Nancy about the head ? If he cannot, he is no bishop, though he had a mitre as high as Salisbury steeple. He is no bishop, — he has sought to be at the helm instead of the masthead; he has no sight of things. "Nay," you say, "it is not his duty to look after Bill in the back street." What ! the fat sheep that have full fleeces, — you think it is only those he should look after, while (go back to your Milton) "the hungry sheep look up, and are not fed, besides what the grim wolf, with privy paw" (bishops knowing nothing about it) "daily devours apace, and nothing said" ?

" But that's not our idea of a bishop." Perhaps not;

but it was St. Paul's, and it was Milton's. They may be right, or we may be ; but we must not think we are reading either one or the other by putting our meaning into their words.

[Ruskin goes on to discuss other expressions with the same minuteness.]

Contributions from Other Studies. — In acquiring any new science or art one learns many new terms, some of which are not too technical for use in themes. For that matter, every exercise written in any subject cannot help being to some extent an exercise in English. The vocabulary book should receive contributions from every line of the student's work.

Translation. — There is no better means of making the memory yield up the words which it has formerly caught, than translation. Professor A. S. Hill quotes the reported .words of Rufus Choate: "Translation should be pursued to bring to mind and to employ all the words you already own, and to tax and torment invention and discovery and the very deepest memory for additional, rich, and admirably expressive words."[1] Every lesson in translating is a lesson in self-expression. Professor Carpenter testifies[2] that the Latin-trained boys entering scientific schools are remarkably superior in power of expression to those not so trained; and his testimony is confirmed by the experience of many other teachers.

[1] *Foundations of Rhetoric*, p. 171.
[2] *Advanced Exercises*, p. 41.

Memorizing of Literature. — To the habit of memorizing, many a person is indebted not merely for high thoughts that cheer hours of solitude and that stimulate his own thinking, but for command of words. The degree to which the language of modern writers is derived from a few great authors is startling. Shakespeare's phrases are a part of the tissue of every man's speech to-day. Such writers as Charles Lamb bear Shakespeare's mark on every page. The language of the King James version of the Bible is echoed in modern English prose and poetry. It formed styles so unlike as those of Bunyan, Ruskin, and Abraham Lincoln. Most teachers would declare that a habit of learning Scripture by heart is of incalculable value to a student's English. In the Authorized Version, and to almost as great an extent in the Revised Version, the Anglo-Saxon element and the Latin are both present in marvellous effectiveness.[1]

It is clear that whatever help one's writing is to receive from memorizing will come naturally through one's study of literature. But so many of the strongest words in the language, particularly the Saxon words, have been treasured up in the homely sayings of the people, that I have ventured to suggest a list of proverbs for memorizing. Just how many of these it may be advisable for a

---

[1] For particular passages, etc., see Professor A. S. Cook's *The Bible and English Prose Style* (Ginn & Co.).

given pupil to retain in mind is a matter to be decided by the instructor. Certainly each student will do well to learn a score of those that seem to him best worth remembering. Each saying preserves some fine word in some natural context, a fact that will-make the word far easier to recall than it would be if learned as an isolated term. Not more than ten or fifteen minutes a day ought to be given to the memorizing.

ENGLISH PROVERBS[1]

A brave retreat is a brave exploit.

A carper can cavil at anything.

A carrion kite will never make a good hawk.

A child is better unborn than untaught.

A custom more honored in the breach than in the observance.

A dogmatical tone, a pragmatical pate.

A diligent scholar, and the master's paid.

A dog's life, hunger and ease.

A dwarf on a giant's shoulders sees farther of the two.

A fair field and no favor.

A fault confessed is half redressed.

A fine new nothing.

A fool always comes short of his reckoning.

A fool will not be foiled.

A forced kindness deserves no thanks.

A good cause makes a stout heart and a strong arm.

A good name keeps its lustre in the dark.

A grain of prudence is worth a pound of craft.

A great city, a great solitude.

[1] Hundreds of others will be found in **Hazlitt's** *English Proverbs*.

A honey tongue, a heart of gall.

A man may buy gold too dear.

A man must sell his ware at the rates of the market.

A man never surfeits of too much honesty.

A nod for a wise man, and a rod for a fool.

A penny saved is a penny got.

A wicked book is the wickeder because it cannot repent.

A wager is a fool's argument.

All complain of want of memory, but none of want of judgment.

All the craft is in the catching.

An unpeaceable man hath no neighbor.

Antiquity is not always a mark of verity.

As wily as a fox.

Better lose a jest than a friend.

Better to go away longing than loathing.

By ignorance we mistake, and by mistakes we learn.

Children are certain cares, but uncertain comforts.

Clowns are best in their own company, but gentlemen are best everywhere.

Conscience cannot be compelled.

Cutting out well is better than sewing up well.

Danger and delight grow on one stock.

Decency and decorum are not pride.

Different sores must have different salves.

Dexterity comes by experience.

Do not spur a free horse.

Even reckoning makes long friends.

Every age confutes old errors and begets **new.**

Every man hath a fool in his sleeve.

Faint praise is disparagement.

Force without forecast is of little avail.

From fame to infamy is a beaten road.

Great businesses turn on a little pin.

Great spenders are bad lenders.

He is lifeless that is faultless.

Heaven will make amends for all.

Let your purse be your master.

*I*dleness is the greatest prodigality in the world.

*I*gnorance is a voluntary misfortune.

*I*t is a wicked thing to make a dearth one's garner.

Lean liberty is better than fat slavery.

Self-love is a mote in every man's eye.

Sloth is the key to poverty.

Some sport is sauce to pains.

Subtility set a trap and caught itself.

Temporizing is sometimes great wisdom.

The goat must browse where he is tied.

The poet, of all sorts of artificers, is the fondest of his works.

The prick of a pin is enough to make an empire insipid.

The purest gold is the most ductile.

There's a craft in daubing.

Thrift is good revenue.

Too much consulting confounds.

Truth needs not many words, but a false tale a large preamble.

Truths too fine-spun are subtle fooleries.

Upbraiding turns a benefit into an injury.

Use your wit as a buckler, not as a sword.

What God made, he never mars.

When honor grew mercenary, money grew honorable.

Where vice is, vengeance follows.

Synonyms. — A synonym is a word that means the same or nearly the same thing as some other word. Our language, from its composite nature, is peculiarly rich in synonyms. In hundreds of cases English has absorbed both the Saxon and the French or Latin word for a given idea. Nearly always, in such cases, one of the words has acquired a distinctly different shade of meaning from the other. Indeed, one of the words is sure to acquire a slightly different *value*, whether from its associations or its sound. While it may roughly be said that there are words which mean the same thing, yet for the really careful writer there are no synonyms.

Synonyms for Adjectives of Praise. — In another sense there are many people who seem to have no synonyms. You have doubtless known persons who lacked all means of differentiating praise, — persons who applied the same adjective to everything, from a pin to the solar system. There are the people who find everything either *nice* or *not nice;* the people who eat *elegant soups* and sigh at *elegant sunsets;* the people who have *jolly times, jolly canes, jolly excuses.* To the *nice* group, the *elegant* group, and the *jolly* group, may be added the *lovely* group, and many others.

Oral Exercise. — Apply several proper adjectives of praise to each of the following: soup, sunset, poodle, lady, moon, time (*e.g.* meaning an excursion), silk, opera, book-binding, gown, face, mountain, box of sweets, ice-cream, disposition, story, manner, soul, fan, perfume, roses, piano-playing, sermon, editorial or leader, critique.

A Danger. — The study of synonyms cultivates discrimination. But as a study for the purpose of widening the active vocabulary it must be judiciously limited. If one turns to a book of synonyms, one finds on many a page some score of words meaning nearly the same thing. Many of these words are unusual, out-of-the-way expressions, to use which would make a man sound like a prig. Simplicity is a cardinal virtue in writing. If this fact is kept in mind, and the student does not affect too elaborate and bookish words, the study of synonyms will be of the utmost service to him.

A Method of Study. — Below are listed a good many groups of synonyms. They are to be studied now and to be used hereafter for reference in the work of writing. Each group contains only a few of the words that might demand a place if the question were merely one of meaning. The words here chosen are such as may properly appear in the work of any high school student, *if there is need of them to express the student's meaning.*

Even in these groups some words are simpler, and therefore in general more desirable. *The class should first examine the entire list, underlining carefully the simpler words in each group. These simpler words are regularly to be preferred when their meaning is exact enough for the idea in mind.* The others are to be mastered for the sake of the distinctions they express, and for their occasional usefulness as a means of avoiding repetitions.

The underlining finished, the groups may further be studied with a view to discriminating the various terms. Fifteen minutes a day is enough to devote to this work, and in some cases it may be best to examine minutely only a part of the list, leaving the rest to be used for reference.

Written Exercise. — It will be found useful to spend five minutes a day in copying off several times each unfamiliar word. Unless the hand is accustomed to tracing the word, the mind will not be likely to demand this act of the hand in the moment of composition.

Oral Exercise. — Each student may be asked to pronounce every word that he has not been in the habit of using orally. Since the same term is likely to have been neglected by many of the class, a considerable amount of ear-training will be received by all.

Oral Exercise. — One of the best, because most natural, ways of studying synonyms, is to examine a page of good prose with a view to seeing whether synonyms could have been used as effectively as the actual words in the text. Choose such a page, underline the important words, and examine the list to find the group to which each belongs. Then substitute for the word in the text the other words of the group, and see whether the author's choice was wise.

Oral Exercise. — Each group should be taken up in turn and discussed by the class after the meanings of unfamiliar words have been looked up in the dictionary. The force of each word *as a synonym of the others in its group* should be brought out by illustrative sentences. The differences in meaning should be talked about until they are thoroughly understood. Fernald's *Synonyms, Antonyms, and Prepositions*, and Smith's *Synonyms Discriminated*, are good books of reference if any doubtful question arises.

Written Exercise. — Study an assigned number of groups, and pick out the word which seems to have the most general meaning, the word which, more than any other, includes the remaining members of the group. Thus, in the series *Actual, authentic, genuine, real*, the last is the most general term. *Real* applies to a larger number of things than any of its synonyms.

Written Exercise. — Study an assigned number of groups, and say what idea the members of each have in common, and, if possible, what additional idea each member has. Thus, *Adept, adroit, deft, dexterous, handy, skilful*, each have the idea *skilful*. *Adept* means skilful in some art or occupation. *Adroit* means skilful with the hand, or with the mind, — *i.e.* tactful. *Deft, dexterous* usually mean skilful with the hand; *deft* refers to movements of the fingers, *dexterous* to quick motions, as of the hand. *Handy* means skilful at manual exercises.

Oral Exercise. — One member of each group should be pronounced, and the student asked to give from memory the other members.

Oral or Written Exercise. — Only one part of speech is represented in each group. The student should be asked to give corresponding parts of speech. Thus, the adjective series *Actual, authentic, genuine, real*, yields the adverbs *actually, authentically, genuinely, really*, and the nouns *actuality, authenticity, genuineness, reality.*

GROUPS OF SYNONYMS[1]

Abandon, cast off, desert, forswear, quit, renounce, withdraw from.

Abate, decrease, diminish, mitigate, moderate.

Abhor, abominate, detest, dislike, loathe.

Abiding, enduring, lasting, permanent, perpetual.

Ability, capability, capacity, competency, efficacy, power.

Abolish, annul, eradicate, exterminate, obliterate, root out, wipe out.

Abomination, curse, evil, iniquity, nuisance, shame.

Absent, absent-minded, absorbed, abstracted, oblivious, preoccupied.

Absolve, acquit, clear.

Abstemiousness, abstinence, frugality, moderation, sobriety, temperance.

[1] For reference: Fallows, *100,000 Synonyms and Antonyms* (Fleming H. Revell Co.); Roget, *Thesaurus;* Fernald, *Synonyms, Antonyms, and Prepositions* (Funk and Wagnalls).

Absurd, ill-advised, ill-considered, ludicrous, monstrous, paradoxical, preposterous, unreasonable, wild.

Abundant, adequate, ample, enough, generous, lavish, plentiful.

Accomplice, ally, colleague, helper, partner.

Active, agile, alert, brisk, bustling, energetic, lively, supple.

Actual, authentic, genuine, real.

Adept, adroit, deft, dexterous, handy, skilful.

Address, adroitness, courtesy, readiness, tact.

Adequate, competent, equal, fitted, suitable.

Adjacent, adjoining, bordering, near, neighboring.

Admire, adore, respect, revere, venerate.

Admit, allow, concede, grant, suffer, tolerate.

Admixture, alloy.

Adverse, disinclined, indisposed, loath, reluctant, slow, unwilling.

Aerial, airy, animated, ethereal, frolicsome.

Affectation, cant, hypocrisy, pretence, sham.

Affirm, assert, avow, declare, maintain, state.

Aged, ancient, antiquated, antique, immemorial, old, venerable.

Air, bearing, carriage, demeanor.

Akin, alike, identical.

Alert, on the alert, sleepless, wary, watchful.

Allay, appease, calm, pacify.

Alliance, coalition, compact, federation, union, fusion.

Allude, hint, imply, insinuate, intimate, suggest.

Allure, attract, cajole, coax, inveigle, lure.

Amateur, connoisseur, novice, tyro.

Amend, better, mend, reform, repair.

Amplify, develop, expand, extend, unfold, widen.

Amusement, diversion, entertainment, pastime.

Anger, exasperation, petulance, rage, resentment.

Animal, beast, brute, living creature, living organism.

Answer, rejoinder, repartee, reply, response, retort.

Anticipate, forestall, preclude, prevent.

Apiece, individually, severally, separately.

Apparent, clear, evident, obvious, tangible, unmistakable.

Apprehend, comprehend, conceive, perceive, understand.

Arraign, charge, cite, impeach, indict, prosecute, summon.

Arrogance, haughtiness, presumption, pride, self-complacency, superciliousness, vanity.

Artist, artificer, artisan, mechanic, operative, workman.

Artless, boorish, clownish, hoidenish, rude, uncouth, unsophisticated.

Assent, agree, comply.

Assurance, effrontery, hardihood, impertinence, impudence, incivility, insolence, officiousness, rudeness.

Atom, grain, scrap, particle, shred, whit.

Atrocious, barbaric, barbarous, brutal, merciless.

Attack, assault, infringement, intrusion, onslaught.

Attain, accomplish, achieve, arrive at, compass, reach, secure.

Attempt, endeavor, essay, strive, try, undertake.

Attitude, pose, position, posture.

Attribute, ascribe, assign, charge, impute.

Axiom, truism.

Baffle, balk, bar, check, embarrass, foil, frustrate, hamper, hinder, impede, retard, thwart.

Banter, burlesque, drollery, humor, jest, raillery, wit, witticism.

Beg, plead, press, urge.

Beguile, divert, enliven, entertain, occupy.

Bewilderment, confusion, distraction, embarrassment, perplexity.

Bind, fetter, oblige, restrain, restrict.

Blaze, flame, flare, flash, flicker, glare, gleam, gleaming, glimmer, glitter, light, lustre, shimmer, sparkle.

Blessed, hallowed, holy, sacred, saintly.

Boasting, display, ostentation, pomp, pompousness, show.

Brave, adventurous, bold, courageous, daring, dauntless, fearless, gallant, heroic, undismayed.

Bravery, coolness, courage, gallantry, heroism.

*B*rief, concise, pithy, sententious, terse.

Bring over, convince, induce, influence, persuade, prevail upon, win over.

*C*alamity, disaster, misadventure, mischance, misfortune mishap.

*C*andid, impartial, open, straightforward, transparent, un-biassed, unprejudiced, unreserved.

*C*aprice, humor, vagary, whim.

*C*andor, frankness, truth, veracity.

*C*aricature, burlesque, parody, travesty.

*C*atch, capture, clasp, clutch, grip, secure.

*C*ause, consideration, design, end, ground, motive, object, reason, purpose.

*C*aution, discretion, prudence.

*C*ensure, criticism, rebuke, reproof, reprimand, reproach.

*C*haracter, constitution, disposition, reputation, temper, temperament.

*C*haracteristic, peculiarity, property, singularity, trait.

*C*hattering, garrulous, loquacious, talkative.

*C*heer, comfort, delight, ecstasy, gaiety, gladness, gratifi-cation, happiness, jollity, satisfaction.

*C*hurlish, crusty, gloomy, gruff, ill-natured, morose, sour, sullen, surly.

*C*lass, circle, clique, coterie.

*C*loak, cover, gloss over, mitigate, palliate, screen.

*C*loy, sate, satiate, satisfy, surfeit.

*C*ommit, confide, consign, entrust, relegate.

*C*ompassion, forbearance, lenience, mercy.

*C*ompassionate, gracious, humane.

*C*omplete, consummate, faultless, flawless, perfect.

*C*onfirm, corroborate.

*C*onflicting, discordant, discrepant, incongruous, mismated.

*C*onfused, discordant, miscellaneous, various.

*C*onjecture, guess, suppose, surmise.

*C*onscious, aware, certain.

*C*onsequence, issue, outcome, outgrowth, result, sequel, upshot.

Continual, continuous, incessant, unbroken, uninterrupted.

Credible, conceivable, likely, presumable, probable, reasonable.

Customary, habitual, normal, prevailing, usual, wonted.

Damage, detriment, disadvantage, harm, hurt, injury, prejudice.

Dangerous, formidable, terrible.

Defame, deprecate, disparage, slander, vilify.

Defile, infect, soil, stain, sully, taint, tarnish.

Deleterious, detrimental, hurtful, harmful, mischievous, pernicious, ruinous.

Delicate, fine, minute, refined, slender.

Delightful, grateful, gratifying, refreshing, satisfying.

Difficult, laborious, toilsome, trying.

Digress, diverge, stray, swerve, wander.

Disavow, disclaim, disown, recall, renounce, repudiate, retract.

Dispose, draw, incline, induce, influence, move, prompt, stir.

Earlier, foregoing, previous, preliminary.

Effeminate, feminine, womanish, womanly.

Emergency, extremity, necessity.

Empty, fruitless, futile, idle, trifling, unavailing, useless, vain, visionary.

Erudition, knowledge, profundity, sagacity, sense, wisdom.

Eternal, imperishable, interminable, perennial, perpetual, unfailing.

Excuse, pretence, pretext, subterfuge.

Exemption, immunity, liberty, license, privilege.

Explicit, express.

Faint, faint-hearted, faltering, half-hearted, irresolute, languid, listless, purposeless.

Faithful, loyal, stanch, trustworthy, trusty.

Fanciful, fantastic, grotesque, imaginative, visionary.

Folly, imbecility, senselessness, stupidity.

Fling, gibe, jeer, mock, scoff, sneer, taunt.

Flock, bevy, brood, covey, drove, herd, litter, pack.

*F*luctuate, hesitate, oscillate, vacillate, waver.

Grief, melancholy, regret, sadness, sorrow.

Hale, healthful, healthy, salutary, sound, vigorous.

*I*gnorant, illiterate, uninformed, uninstructed, unlettered, untaught.

*I*mpulsive, involuntary, spontaneous, unbidden, voluntary, willing.

*I*ndispensable, inevitable,. necessary, requisite, unavoidable.

*I*nquisitive, inquiring, 'intrusive, meddlesome, peeping, prying.

*I*ntractable, perverse, petulant, ungovernable, wayward, wilful.

*I*rritation, offence, pique, resentment.

Probably, presumably.

Reliable, trustworthy, trusty.

Remnant, trace, token, vestige.

Requite, repay, retaliate, satisfy.

Oral or Written Exercise. — In the following, vary the overworked words as much as possible. Permit repetition only when it is necessary for clearness.

1. I think the committee selected to select theme topics for the class to write upon, should be careful not to select too many topics on one subject, since the nature of one student differs from that of another. I think that the few who are not satisfied with the topics the committee have selected, should be required to select and hand in a list of topics on which they would like to write.

2. There are two distinct stories running through the Merchant of Venice: the story of the pound of

flesh and the story of the caskets. These stories run parallel to each other through the play, as far as the third act, where the story of the caskets is ended by the lucky choice of Bassanio. But from here a new story, the story of the rings, commenees, and continues through the rest of the play, crossing the story of the pound of flesh and finally taking the place of this story.

Future Revision. — Henceforth one distinct object for which every theme should be revised is *variety of words.* It soon becomes a keen satisfaction to read one's own work aloud to detect overworked expressions. In the pursuit of variety, the scholar not merely grows sensitive to the ugly recurrence of the same sound; he grows bold to repeat words if the repetition is demanded for clearness or force. Some things seem to have but one name in English; more's the pity; but we must make the best of the case.

CHAPTER XI

RIGHT NUMBER AND SKILFUL CHOICE OF WORDS

Let it be supposed that a person has learned to plan a composition logically and to write with grammatical correctness; that further he has acquired a noble unrest which keeps him searching for new words and fine distinctions; what should be his next care?

After the power of thinking coherently, the ability most important to a writer is that of picking out from the wide world of words the one expression that mates his unworded idea. His choice of words — *i.e.* his *diction* — must meet three requirements. If it is to be *clear*, it must mean the same to the reader's intellect that it does to the writer's. If it is to be *forcible*, it must move the reader's feelings as it moved the writer's. Furthermore, if it is to be *beautiful*, it must please a reader who has good taste.

Clearness. — Clearness, the intellectual quality of style, has already been referred to (p. 43), for it is the quality aimed at in making sentences coherent.

That the idea should be made unmistakably clear is the first requisite of good writing. The thinking must be clear; the division of the theme into paragraphs, and of paragraphs into sentences must be clear; and the words must be clear. We have presently to ask what effect number and choice of words have upon clearness.

Force. — Force is the emotional quality of style. It may occur in a very moderate degree, just enough to *interest* the reader slightly, or it may be present to such an extent as to move the deepest springs of feeling. It is hard to give suggestions for securing force, because language is better adapted to communicating ideas than emotions. We find that language furnishes very few names for feelings. Furthermore, these names, even such as *love, fear, anger*, do not in themselves move us. What a marvellous variety of emotion each of us feels in a day! how many delicate tints of pleasure! how many shades of regret or fear, of painful memory or suggestion! The psychologists tell us that we do no act which does not bring with it some touch of pleasure or of pain. And yet most of these shades and tints and touches of feeling neither have names nor can be communicated by words. Nevertheless, though language cannot directly convey feeling, it can sometimes suggest feeling. If your reader has experienced a given emotion, some word of yours may recall that to his mind. One secret of being forcible lies in choosing theme subjects that interest the reader; subjects that set up a train of feeling and memory in his mind. Other secrets are, to choose *suggestive* words and figures of speech, and to refrain from wearing out interest by too many words. We shall presently inquire, what words and figures are most suggestive.

Something may be done to secure force by so arranging words as to attract the reader's attention. It will be noted that emphasis (p. 110) and climax (p. 112) are means of force.

Beauty. — Beauty is the quality of style which satisfies what is called, for lack of a better word, the æsthetic sense; this is little else but saying, beauty of style satisfies the sense for beauty. One element of beauty is *simplicity*, a quality closely allied to clearness, yet not the same. *Euphony*, or absence of ugly sounds, is another element of beauty. *Variety* is another element of beauty. It is clear that the last exercise in Chapter X is as much an exercise in beauty as in vocabulary. In the present chapter we shall have space to consider only one element of beauty, — that of simplicity.

Prolixity. — If a writer descends into tedious details, or if he repeats the same idea over and over in slightly different words, without developing or adding to the thought, he is said to be prolix. Prolixity offends chiefly against force, for it kills interest. This fault may affect merely a single sentence or paragraph, or it may infest a whole composition. It does not much beset the writer who plans his work ahead. It can be corrected only by rewriting.

Written Exercise. — The following prolix passage should be rewritten, only the essential thoughts being kept. Any mistakes and crudities of style should be corrected.

"My friend the doctor was a collector of ancient coins and was always roaming about the ruins of old cities in search of coins. He would wander around and pick up valuable relics like the Venus he wore in his seal ring. He was always finding something worth keeping. He would pick up a precious bit of antiquity and put it in his pocket, and so he always carried with him a regular collection of relics. One afternoon he was out among the mountains picking up relics and not looking up to see whether any one was near. When he looked around he saw five or perhaps six rough fellows who were standing there behind him. He fell to quivering with fright and stood trembling and shaking, but managed to greet them. After he had greeted the five or six men they all walked along down the road until they came to an inn that was there on the mountain-side. It was an inn and not a cave there in the mountains, as was incorrectly said by one member of the class."

Surplusage. — Surplusage consists of words that can be excised without hurting the sense of the passage. In tyros it is perhaps less of a fault than the opposite one of *deficiency,* — the absence of needed words; for fulness of expression is essential to clearness, and surplusage often results from the desire to be clear. Verbosity, however, dulls the edge of the keenest thought. Like prolixity, it weakens. Just as many a prolix speaker could make a brilliant oration if he knew when to stop, so many a wordy writer could make an effective sentence if he knew what to prune away. As Mr. Lowell would say:[1] Thoughts are never draped in long skirts like babies, if they are strong enough to go alone.

The redundant use of the following common words should be avoided : —

1. *From,* in the phrases *from thence, from whence.*

2. *Of,* especially in the expressions *off of, remember of, treat of.* "Keep off [not *off of*] the grass." "This book treats [better than *treats of*] chemistry."

3. *On,* with the words *the next morning.* "He was rebellious on the seventh of July, but the next

[1] *Among My Books,* II. 259.

morning [not *on the next morning*] he reappeared in a more submissive frame of mind."

Oral Exercise. — Prune away every word that can be spared; note the increase in force. Slight changes may be made in the wording.

1. All of the ships were lost; no kind of a one was saved.

2. I know from my own personal knowledge that a man who stands upright in his own manhood, honest and conscious of the rectitude of his purposes, is safe against calumny and slander.

3. I don't think it a good precedent to set in this house for any man to vote for a bill in which he has a personal interest, and I don't remember of ever having done so of myself. I shall, therefore, for this reason, refrain from voting, but I want to say a word on this bill, and I want to talk to the democrats.

4. Real-estate dealer is knocked down by an accident and is run over by a cab.

5. Commencing on Monday, March 29, supported by the New York Garrick Theatre Stock Company, Mr. Mansfield will commence an engagement of two weeks at the Grand Opera House.

Written or Oral Exercise. — In the following sentences some of the underscored expressions should be expressed more briefly by changing clauses to phrases or phrases to single words.

Thus: *men who deserved and won renown* may shorten to *men of deserved renown.*

1. *Men who deserved and won renown,* and *women who were peerless,* have lived upon what we should now call the coarsest fare, and paced the rushes *which were strewn* in their rooms with as high, or as contented thoughts, as their *descendants, persons who are fed better and clothed better than they,* can boast of.

2. If children *are able* to make us wiser, *it is sure that they can also* make us better. There is no one *who is more to be envied* than a good-natured man *when he is watching how children's minds perform their workings, or when he is overlooking the play they engage in.*

Deficiency of Words. — It was said in a former paragraph that in young writers surplusage is perhaps less of a fault than is the lack of needed words. Verbosity robs a theme of force; deficiency robs it of force and clearness. It is human nature to try to say a thing more briefly than is possible. Forgetting that pitch, stress, and gesture do much to make spoken words intelligible, the easy-going writer does not tax himself to attain full and lucid expression. He forgets that a piece of writing may be so condensed as to be dense.

Ambiguity often springs from the omission of merely a word or two. Reading such a phrase as "the secretary and treasurer," we are vexed with doubt whether one person is meant, or two; the omission of the article seems to imply that the two offices are vested in a single officer. The lack of a few words may turn force into weakness. A German newspaper thus burlesques the compression to which editors sometimes feel impelled: "Ottokar took a small brandy, then his hat, his departure, besides no notice of his pursuers, meantime a revolver out of his pocket, and lastly his own life."

The following common words should not be omitted: —

1. The main part of an infinitive at the end of a sentence. *Wrong:* "He did what he wished to." *Right:* "He did what he wished to do."

2. The adverb *much* before certain adjectives. *Wrong:* "He was very pleased to comply." *Right:* "He was very much pleased to comply."

3. (*a*) The preposition *at* with home. *Wrong:* "I stayed home and slept home." *Right:* "I stayed at home and slept at home." (*b*) The preposition *on* with days of the month. *Wrong:* "The seventh of July he rebelled." *Right:* "On the seventh of July he rebelled." Compare page 231. 3.

4. A demonstrative used for clearness. *Wrong:* "He chose between the lot of the rich and of the poor." *Right:* "He chose between the lot of the rich and that of the poor."

5. The conjunction *that* when needed for clearness. *Wrong:* " I wish such a beefsteak as that one over there may never be served on this table." What is the ambiguity here, at the beginning ?

Oral Exercise. — Indicate how by the addition of words each sentence may be corrected : —

1. Altogether it was a day like unto which the memory of the oldest inhabitant could not recall.

2. He received his early education at Brownsville and Whitesville academy, remaining about a year at each place.

3. There was a minister who, being informed by the church officials that they had raised his salary $100, declined to accept it.

4. The following great reductions indicate the heavy losses we are taking closing out the balance of our stock.

5. This mutual esteem was shown by their cordial welcome of the guests as well as the uniform courtesy shown by the latter.

6. Poor Evelina was obliged to choose between a blue and green dress.

7. Streaks of lightning and claps of thunder rattled through the narrow streets of Paris.

8. I am an historical painter by profession, and living for some time at a villa near Rome.

Specific Words. — Suppose it were desired to make clear to a friend how the sunset looked — a difficult task. One would hardly succeed if one had no better words to offer than the general terms *clouds, beautiful, lovely, bright.* The friend, if he cared to know, would insist on specific words: What kind of beauty? was it quiet beauty, or awful beauty, or picturesque beauty? What kind of brightness? was it redness? If so, was the sky blood-red, or merely pink? What kind of clouds? — great masses of storm cloud, or high frozen clouds, or mottled "mackerel" clouds? To be clear, then, words must be specific enough to give the idea intended. Just how specific they should be depends on the audience. They must be familiar to the hearer or reader, if they are to be understood without explanation. All audiences would understand the general term *tool;* all would understand the genus name *saw,* which specifies a kind of tool. But many would not understand the species name *rip-saw;* for to most people *rip-saw* is unfortunately a technical term. In choosing specific words the line should therefore be drawn between common terms and technical terms, the latter not to be employed without explanation, except in addressing special audiences.

Specific words are usually as forcible as they are clear. Most people's feelings are roused by the thought of a particular object, not of a class name. *Flower* is a class name; it does not move one. *Clover* is a specific name; it calls back the old farm, the old friends, the old joys and sorrows. No word will really interest the reader unless he has previously used it or heard it in association with his feelings. Take the word *contusion;* it means something forcible to a doctor, but not to a boy, for the latter never used it. But say *bruise* — which means exactly the same thing. That's forcible. It feelingly reminds us of the hour in which that dead branch broke and delivered us over to the law of gravitation.

Pick out from these words those that are in themselves forcible to most people: paternal solicitude, fatherly care; home, domicile; altruism, unselfishness. You see at once that certain of these words get their force from the long associations of childhood. In childhood we use the simpler words of the language, those that are derived from the Anglo-Saxon mother-tongue. Anglo-Saxon words, therefore, are usually forcible. Compare page 183.

Oral Exercise. — Reduce the following names step by step to a particular genus and a particular species. Thus: animal, mammal, quadruped, graminivorous animal, cow, Alderney.

1. Reduce *machine* step by step till you reach *stop-watch.*
2. Reduce *machine* to *revolver.*
3. Reduce *living organism* to *moss-rose.*

4. Reduce *living organism* to *oyster.*

Similarly, extend the following species names step by step to family names.

1. Extend *pen-knife* to *instrument.*
2. Extend *Longfellow* to *man of letters.*

General Words. — We found that most specific words are of Anglo-Saxon origin. Most general words are of Latin origin. Both these statements are only roughly true, of course; but the distinction is worth making. The language of science is mostly of Latin origin, because it consists so largely of class names. Our Anglo-Saxon forefathers had fewer class names, for they had not progressed far enough to care to classify everything. When, later, the English came to study history, and philosophy, and science, they had either to invent new Anglo-Saxon words for class names, or else use Latin words. They chose the latter course. Consequently we have such Latin class names as *animal,* and such individual names as *cat, dog, horse, pig.* We speak of *white, blue, green, red ;* but when we want a class name for these, we say *color,* a Latin word. From all this it may be seen that any great number of general words gives a scientific, abstract tone to writing. General words are absolutely necessary for the exact purposes of science and philosophy. They are adapted, as Professor Carpenter puts it, to " precise and elaborate distinctions of thought." They do not give a clear mental image; that is, you cannot *see* beauty, or smallness, or animal, or color — you can see only a beautiful object, a small object, a particular animal, a particular color. But, still, general words mean exactly what they say. *Animal* means exactly this: a summing up of all the qualities that are common to all individual animals. All the things called animal have in common powers of sensation and voluntary movement. When such a distinction is wanted, it is wanted badly, as we say. There is no better mark of literary mastery than knowing just when to use a general word, just when a specific one. Examine a few pages from Robert Louis Stevenson to see with what exquisite fitness words of Latin origin may be used in the midst of Anglo-Saxon words when the appeal turns from the feel ings to the intellect.

There are many reasons why a writer may not wish to be too specific. In the sentence, " I picked up my traps and left," the colloquialism *traps* answers every essential purpose. The reader does not care to have tooth-brush and books and papers all specified. People are not to be blamed for referring vaguely to *death* as a *passing away,* for the specific word is harsh at best. Such expressions as *pass away* are called *euphemisms.* Many euphemisms are legitimate; but whether a given one should be employed is a question of taste, a question of beauty. It seems a beautiful expression when Keats says, "to cease upon the midnight with no pain," instead of, "to die painlessly at twelve o'clock;" but it is a mark of false modesty and bad taste to insist on saying *rose* for *got up, retire* for *go to bed, lower limbs* for *legs.*

Again, one should not always hesitate to set down an idea because one has not the sharpest, clearest possible notion of it. Vague ideas are sometimes valuable ones. They should receive earnest thought that they may take definite shape. But if they seem to defy definite form, they certainly should not be thrown away merely for that. Catching one's exact idea is often as difficult as catching a trout. But a glimpse of the fine fish that gets away is worth something, — there are few of us who can resist the temptation to tell about it when we get home. Speaking of the mind, Emerson says, "It is wholesome to angle in those profound pools, though one be rewarded with nothing more than the leap of a fish that flashes his freckled side in the sun and as suddenly absconds in the dark and dreamy waters again." [1] In Wordsworth's poem, The Solitary Reaper, we hear of a song about *old, unhappy, far-off things.* That was exactly Wordsworth's own vague notion, and down he set it — in words that make it clear

---

[1] Quoted in a different connection by E. E. Hale, Jr., *Constructive Rhetoric,* p. 288 (Henry Holt & Co.).

(so to speak) that his idea was sweet and vague. Ruskin, describing the façade of St. Mark's in Venice, tries to give a sense of the bewildering multiplicity of beautiful things on that wonderful front by saying, *a confusion of delight.* If he had used more definite words we should have missed the effect.

Oral Exercise. — Examine the passages from Johnson and Blackmore (pp. 192–3). Which passage contains more of general words than of specific? Which is more forcible in subject-matter? Which in *diction.*

Oral Exercise. — In the following passage, choose the better expression from each pair of brackets. Each pair contains one general and one specific term; choose the term which gives greater force or greater clearness than the other.

1. And therefore, first of all, I tell you earnestly and authoritatively (I *know* I am right in this) you must get into the [way, habit] of looking [rightly, intensely] at words, and [telling, assuring] yourself of their meaning, syllable by syllable — nay, letter by letter. For . . . you might read all the books in [a great library, the British Museum] (if you could live long enough) and remain an utterly " illiterate," uneducated person; but if you read [some part, ten pages] of [a good, an instructive] book, letter by letter — that is to say, with real [care,

R

accuracy]—you are forevermore in some [way, measure] an educated [man, person]. The entire difference between education and non-education (as regards the merely [mental, intellectual] part of it) consists in this [exactitude, accuracy]. A well-educated gentleman may not [read, know] many languages, may not be able to speak any but his own, may have read very few books. But whatever language he knows, he knows [well, precisely]; whatever word he [says, pronounces] he [says, pronounces] rightly. Above all, he is learned in the *peerage* of words, knows the words of [true, veritable] descent, and [old, ancient] blood, at a glance, from the words of [new, modern] *canaille*, remembers all their ancestry, their intermarriages, distant relationships, and the extent to which they were admitted, and offices they held, among the national *noblesse* of words at any time and in any [place, country]. But an uneducated person may know, by [heart, memory], many languages, and [use, talk] them all, and yet truly [know, apprehend] not a word of any — not a word even of his own. An ordinarily [clever, good] and sensible seaman will be able to make his way ashore at most [ports, places], yet he has only to speak [a little, a sentence] of [Spanish or French, any language] to be [known, recognized] for an illiterate person; so also the accent, or turn of expression of a single sentence, will at once mark a scholar.

And this is so [well, strongly] felt, so [conclusively, well] admitted, by educated persons, that a false accent or a [bad, mistaken] syllable is enough in the parliament of any civilized nation, to [assign, send] man to a certain degree of [lower, inferior] standing forever.

Oral Exercise. — Which words in the following are general, which specific? Does each seem appropriate in its place, or ought some words to have been more specific, others more general?

1. Her dress was dark and rich; she had pearls round her neck, and an old rococo fan in her hand. — HENRY JAMES.

2. When gratitude has become a matter of reasoning, there are many ways of escaping from its bonds. — GEORGE ELIOT.

3. Friendships begin with liking or gratitude — roots that can be pulled up. — GEORGE ELIOT.

4. What scene was ever commonplace in the descending sunlight, when color has awakened from its noonday sleep, and the long shadows awe us like a disclosed presence? Above all, what scene is commonplace to the eye that is filled with serene gladness, and brightens all things with its own joy? — GEORGE ELIOT.

Oral Exercise. — Is there danger of misconception from the use of the following words? If so how can the danger be avoided? Discuss in class.

Fair, fine, certain, charity, democratic, republican, nature.

Simple Words. — Several years ago a gentleman [1] secured from a large number of successful authors brief pieces of advice to young writers. In one particular there was an extraordinary unanimity among these authors. Nearly all agreed that a young writer should try to express himself simply. They agreed on other matters too, — for example, on the need of clear thinking and an inclination to take much pains in expression. But it was noticeable that even writers whose own work is not characterized by simplicity seemed to admire this quality.

The greatest men are simple. Affectation, straining for effect, is a mark of a little mind. The greatest art is simple, — governed by a noble restraint. Over-decoration, whether in a picture, a piece of music, in dress, in the furnishing of a room, or in a theme, is always a mark of bad taste.

What is called fine writing — the use of over-ambitious words to express simple thoughts — grows up in various ways. Sometimes it springs from a desire to be funny. Exaggeration has always been a favorite device of the humorist — especially

[1] Mr. George Bainton, *The Art of Authorship* (D. Appleton & Co.).

of the American humorist. There are students who learn to use this kind of humor so well that an unconscious habit of bombast pursues them into their more serious work. Most of us can force a smile at such writing as the passage given below, or even laugh at it when there are enough people present to help us : —

"It was in the sixth that Captain Anson, aided and abetted by sundry young men generally called 'Colts,' waded in to snatch laurel, trailing arbutus, and other vegetables from the coy hand of fame. He did it, too, and he now has laurels to throw to the birds. Ryan went first to the bat, and pasted a warm one through short that turned the grass black along its path.

But when a young fellow has read so much of this sort that he drags similar diction into his themes, the fun becomes vulgarity.

In general, use always the simplest word that will express your meaning exactly. Compare pages **216, 217.**

Written Exercise. — Write in simple English the equivalents of the following passages. Some are from students' themes; others from newspapers.

1. The *svelte*[1] young debutante received a perfect ovation.

2. In my estimation it is far more to be desired

---

[1] Consult a French dictionary.

that a tyro in the art of composition should select those subjects with which his acquaintance is the most extensive.

3. In all my experience I have never enjoyed the acquaintance of two youths of more superior ability.

4. It is impossible for me to disassociate from my mind the conception that such a course would be disastrous to the ambitions of the team.

5. Public sentiment would not permit an individual or an infinitesimally small minority to clog the wheels of progress in order to prevent the escape of a few dollars from the individuals composing the obstructive element.

6. Let us indeed refrain from any course of action which will militate against the onward march of the civilizing power of the public schools of this great and growing nation.

7. While the birds were carolling their sweetest strains and the grass hung heavy with water-pearls, Peter Brant was taking his life. A more seductive place to die in than the little garden back of 7000 Congress street is inconceivable.

Literal and Figurative Words. — Before it can be decided how far the young writer should use figures of speech, it is necessary to find out the real difference between a literal word or statement and a figurative word or statement. If figures are always mere embellishments of language, the journeyman had better shun them anxiously; for his true object is to express his thought, not to decorate it. If, however, some figures are not embellishments but ordinary building-material, the case is different.

When, on seeing biscuits for the first time, a child refers to them as *moons*, he is not making an effort to adorn his language. He is unconsciously using a figure of speech because he does not know the literal, proper, conventional name, *biscuit*. If the child had formerly lived in a country where apples grew but potatoes did not, the first time he saw a potato he would probably call it a *ground-apple*. As a matter of fact there are people that have gone through some such experience with potatoes. The French word *pomme de terre* indicates this.

Most words were once figures of speech, that is, *tropes*. A trope, from the Greek word τρέπω, to turn, is merely the turning away of a word from its ordinary meaning to give a name to some new idea. The root of many a word shows the figure that was used to express a given new idea. The root *spir-* means to breathe. Since the inability to breathe is one part of the process of death, the expression *to breathe out* became a figurative expression for the whole idea of "to die." In *expire*, applied to death, the idea of *breathe* is usually not felt. The figure is forgotten, and we therefore call it a root-figure, or *radical figure.* As may be seen from the roots of the Curious Words on page 191, language is figurative through and through.

This is true not only of language already made, but of that which is daily making. In every mind shades of thought are constantly occurring for which there are either no names, or none which the mind can learn in the interval before expression is necessary. If the exact word is not at hand, a comparison must be made. The shade of thought must be named by telling what thing in the reader's experience it is like.

Does the attempt at comparison result in a vague, inexact phrase, or in an exact one ? The youth who declares that his lesson is as " hard as thunder," has expressed himself but vaguely. The same is true of the young lady who declares that it rained "like anything." Let us examine briefly the chief kinds of tropes, and note whether they are necessarily less clear and exact than literal statements.

A person sees an accident, and reports that " a score of hands " picked up the injured boy. Here is *synecdoche.* The " hands " stand for the persons — a part for the whole; a " score " probably stands for a dozen, — the whole number of hands in the group of people, for the smaller number that actually touched the boy. Or, the " score " may be called *hyperbole*, that is, exaggeration. A critic might say that either figure is inexact here. True, in a way. But if the writer had reported that he *seemed* to see a score of hands, the phrase would be faithful to his thought. We may take the *seemed* for granted, and reply to the critic that for exact purposes in a law court, "seemed to see a score of hands" might be nearer the truth than an attempt at greater precision.

Suppose, now, that the writer who reported the accident said that the boy was in great pain, so that his face was "as white as ivory." Here is a *simile*, — an explicit statement of likeness in two things which are different in most respects. This particular simile is certainly more exact than the literal word *white* would be.

If now the writer had said, " I caught a glimpse of compressed lips and ivory face," the comparison would have been not explicit, but implied. An implied comparison is called *metaphor*. Metaphor is from the Greek for *carrying over*, because it carries over bodily the name of one thing to another. To speak of a man as " bold as a lion," is simile; to call him a " lion " outright, is metaphor. It is less clear to call a man a lion than to say in what respect he is like a lion; it is less clear to say, " ivory face " than to say " face white as ivory."

The case of the boy who was injured may have got into the newspapers. To speak more figuratively, the *press* may have taken up the matter. *Press* stands here for the editors of the various journals. This last figure is *metonymy*. In metonymy one thing is put for another that is often associated with it. In the sentence given, metonymy does not seem to detract from clearness; at all events it saves a roundabout expression.

Metaphor and metonymy, by ascribing life to inanimate things, often become *personification*. So above, where the press *takes up* a matter. It is evident that personification need not make a sentence less intelligible.

Once more, let us suppose that the reporter who first learned of the boy's accident remarked, on handing in his account of it, "The early bird catches the worm." The remark is pure *allegory* — describing some act or thing indirectly by describing something else. If the hearer knows enough of the situation to understand the allegory, he undoubtedly receives a forcible impression, and may be helped to a clearer view. Allegory is a kind of expanded metaphor. It is more liable to misinterpretation than most figures; but the allegorical proverbs of our language, and the popularity of such books as the *Pilgrim's Progress*, show that it is a favorite form of expression. Like general words, allegory can be used to say things which policy may forbid being said more directly.

From the discussion it appears that tropes can

often be made to yield a clear and sufficiently exact phrase. Often however a trope lends force or beauty rather than clearness. It is forcible rather than clear to call a man a lion. It is beautiful rather than clear to speak of the Pleiades as "a swarm of fireflies tangled in a silver braid." Such a phrase as this is legitimate enough in poetry; it would be legitimate in highly imaginative prose. But the fact cannot be dodged that it would be out of place in the midst of plain prose description.

The practical conclusion is obvious. Use tropes without hesitation when they are really needed to give clearness and force. Never use a trope for decorative purposes only. The ability to write plain, bare English is absolutely indispensable. The ability to write figuratively is an enviable, but not a necessary, possession.

When the need of a figure is actually felt, the choice should be made with scrupulous care. If tropes occur to you in numbers, "like flocks of pigeons," choose only the pigeon that can carry a message. To secure lucidity, employ a figure which makes use of something already clear to the reader. Every-day life and common things are the best sources for both similes and metaphors. To secure force, select such figures as appeal to the emotional experiences of everybody. If you wish to hold attention and move your reader, appeal to such primal feelings as love, hate, fear, courage, joy, sorrow, aspiration, hope. Note how Shakespeare appeals to the human animal's dread of deep water : he makes Cardinal Wolsey say, " I have ventured, like wanton boys that swim on bladders, this many summers in a sea of glory." In *Macbeth* he appeals to the joy of release from pain: he calls sleep *the balm* of each day's hurt.

A good figure of speech must be consistent. Although a lively imagination changes its metaphors from minute to minute, it must not change them so fast as to suggest ridiculous things. If the metaphor gets mixed, clearness and force go to the winds. The other day the writer heard a young man earnestly exclaim: " Now I shall have to toe the bee-line!" The thought of that youth, lifted to a perilous position where his toes sought vainly in the trackless air for a " bee-line," was quite too much for the gravity of his hearers. This trope that failed to be a trope was about as effective as the famous lightning-change series of metaphors uttered by Sir Boyle Roche: " Mr. Speaker, I smell a rat. I see him floating in the air. But I will nip him in the bud." Mixed metaphors may arise from mere liveliness of imagination, — a good fault sometimes. More frequently it arises from vague thinking or from grandiloquence. The examples on page 246 show how liable fine writing is to this fault. A figure that is not in good taste is incomparab*l*y worse than no figure at all.

Oral Exercise. — Name each trope, and explain how each gets its force ; what emotion each touches.

(*a*) " Thy soul was like a star and dwelt apart." — WORDSWORTH.

(*b*) " What is hope ? — a smiling rainbow children fol*l*ow through the wet." — CARLYLE.

(*c*) " She speaks poniards, and every word stabs." — SHAKESPEARE.

(*d*) " B*l*iss was it in that dawn to be alive ; but to be young was very heaven." — WORDSWORTH.

(*e*) " Prayer is the key of the morning and the bolt of the night." — BEECHER.

Oral Exercise. — Examine the phrases that you made by finding adjectives to fit abstract qualities (p. 202), and decide in each case whether clearness or force is the chief resulting characteristic.

Oral Exercise. — Restore force to the following figures by changing whatever is incongruous in them. Reject any that are irretrievably bad in taste, or hackneyed.

1. The singing was led by the organ assisted by four violins.

2. In graceful and figurative language he pointed the finger of scorn at the defendant.

3. It was 8 o'clock when the guests attacked the following menu.

4. The trailer struck the car amidships.

5. The colonies were not yet ripe to bid adieu to British connection.

6. Let us cast off the shackles of doubt and bind ourselves with the bonds of faith.

7. No human happiness is so serene as not to contain some alloy.

8. Boyle was the father of chemistry, and brother of the Earl of Cork.

9. The marble-hearted marauder might seize the throne of civil authority, and hurl into thraldom the votaries of rational liberty.

10. It is to be hoped, now that lovely woman discountenances the flowing bowl, that the rising generation will abjure it, and follow the weaker sex in taking nothing stronger than the cup which cheers but not inebriates.

CHAPTER XII

LETTER-WRITING

Why Important. — There are two general classes of letters: informal or personal, and formal or impersonal. Each kind is governed by the general principles of clearness and courtesy. Mischief is sure to follow if either of these principles is disregarded. A writer may indulge in extravagance of statement when he writes for the public, and "there is no harm done, for the speaker is one and the listener is another."[1] But it is quite a different matter when one is making business promises, or trying to pacify a distant friend with whom there is a misunderstanding. A shrewd politician knows enough not to write too many letters, and not to write anything that he cannot stand by. A woman of tact knows that the success of her social plans may turn upon the choice of a single word in the leave-taking of a note.

Business Letters. — These are formal, impersonal. A good business letter is (1) clear, (2) courteous,

[1] The Turkish Cadi to the English Traveller. See James, *Psychology*, II. 640.

(3) brief. It shows unmistakably (*a*) who is writing, (*b*) to whom, (*c*) where, (*d*) when. It is definite in its language, so that there need be no return letter of inquiry as to any part of its meaning. It observes the best conventions of address and signature. It refrains from brusque remarks, even in reply to a rude letter. It is appreciative. A good business man always takes into account that a handful of trade is a handful of gold; if he is favored with orders, he goes to the trouble of thanking his customers. It does not curtly abbreviate sentences and signatures. Life is not so short but that we may avoid writing such insults as this: "Y'rs rec'd and contents noted. Have ordered Jones to push the deal through. Shall see you soon. Y'rs respy."

Headings and Signatures in Business Letters. — A business letter should show where it was written, and where the answer should be sent. If these places are the same, the one address may be indicated either at the beginning or at the end, preferably the former. Street and number should always be given in the case of city addresses. The date of writing should be placed at the beginning, the month being written or abbreviated, not indicated by a figure. The heading ought also to indicate to whom the letter is sent. Since in theory or in fact there may be other persons of the same name, the correspondent's address should usually be placed beneath his name. The most common signatures in business letters are *Yours truly, Yours very truly,* and *Yours respectfully.* In writing a business letter, a girl signs her full name. Then at the left she writes her name, preceded by *Miss,* and followed by her address.

Titles in Business Letters. — Firm names need not be preceded by *Messrs.,* although this form certainly adds to the courtesy of the communication. Names of individuals should regularly be preceded by *Mr.* Whether a person should be addressed by his professional title depends somewhat upon the character of the business. *In the United States a commercial letter is sufficiently courteous if **Mr.** precedes the name of the person addressed.* This title. is in better taste, as applied to business men, than *Esq.* But there is no objection to the use of certain titles, and they are desirable if the business be one which pertains to the profession of the person addressed. Initials should always be given. "Rev. Brown" "Hon. Jones," are inexcusable forms.

The Envelope. — The address on the envelope should be as legible as possible. Names of states should not be contracted. As Professor J. M. Hart remarks, "The only current abbreviations that seem to be safe are Penna., Conn., and D. C." [1] New

---

[1] *Handbook of English Composition,* p. 348 (Eldredge & Bro.).

s

York City may be written for New York, N. Y.
The same rules for titles apply to the envelope
as to the heading. If the comma is placed after
one line of the address, it must be placed after the
others. It is needed after none.

Written Exercise. — Write a business letter, re-
plying clearly and courteously to the following
imaginary communication.

14 Grasmere Street,
Boston, Mass.,
Dec. 4, 1897.

Miss Helen Roe,
    Graysville, Penna.
Dear Madam : —

We beg to acknowledge the receipt of your
order of Dec. 2. Since you mention the fact that
the goods are intended as a Christmas surprise,
we have taken the liberty of holding them, and
writing for orders as to desired date of shipment
to the address you specify. We remain,

Very respectfully yours,
Weaver and Weaver.

Written Exercise. — Write a petition to some
person or persons in authority, following in general
the form given below : —

The Faculty of Lewis Institute.

Gentlemen : We, the undersigned, respectfully
ask the privilege of organizing a new literary

society, to be called the Parnassian. We enclose a copy of the proposed constitution, which we are ready to sign. If further information is desired, we shall be glad to appoint a committee to wait upon you at any time you may designate.

L. Gustafson,
H. Bulkley, etc.

Formal Social Letters. — Formal correspondence indicates by its style the mere acquaintance of the correspondents, or, in the words of Miss Morton,[1] " the bounds of distance which for any reason it is desirable to maintain." A formal letter should actually be formal. If one attempts to do an elaborate thing, one ought to do it thoroughly and properly. A letter that begins with formal brevity and runs off into colloquial prolixity is a burlesque. A letter that begins in the third person and ends in the first is a farce.

Written Exercise. — Following in general the models given below, write (1) a formal invitation to dinner; (2) an acceptance of this invitation; (3) regrets at inability to accept.

1. Mr. Frederick Estoff, Jr., requests the pleasure of Mr. Edward Edwards' company at dinner on Tuesday, June fourth, at seven o'clock, to meet Mr. and Mrs. Frederick Estoff.

12 Pear Street, June twenty-eighth.

---

[1] *Letter-Writing*, p. 121 (Penn. Pub. Co.).

2. Mr. Edward Edwards accepts with much pleasure the kind invitation of Mr. Frederick Estoff, Jr., to dinner for June fourth, to meet Mr. and Mrs. Frederick Estoff.

14 Sycamore Street, June twenty-eighth.

3. Mr. Edward Edwards regrets extremely that a previous engagement prevents his acceptance of Mr. Frederick Estoff, Jr.'s kind invitation to dinner for June fourth, to meet Mr. and Mrs. Frederick Estoff.

14 Sycamore Street, June twenty-eighth.

Personal or Informal Letters. — The letter one writes informally to an acquaintance, a friend, or a relative, should be in tone pretty nearly what one's conversation with the given person would be. To give such a letter the tone which represents exactly the relation between the two people is a hard task. The nicest sense of tact is required in order not to be too stiff and not too familiar. Personal letters demand the art of colloquial composition. Those unperceptive persons who have but one style of composition, — that of a book, or that of a clerk, — make sorry work of personal letters. Suppose that you have always known one of these persons. You have played with him, read with him, perhaps fought with him. When you meet, he calls you by your first name. When he writes to ask you to visit him, he addresses you as *Dear Sir,* and signs himself *Respectfully!* His letter gives you a chill. There is too little of the personal letter-writting of the better sort, the leisurely, careful, courteous, old-fashioned kind of written talk, — writing that, like Thomas Cholmondeley's, could be signed, " Ever yours and not in haste."

Written Exercise. —Write a note inviting a friend of your own age to dinner, to an informal party, or to an excursion. Such a note usually begins on this wise, — *My Dear Tom,* or *Dear Tom,* rather than on this, — *Dear Friend.* A similar note to an acquaintance would begin: My dear Mr. ——, My dear Miss ——, etc.

Written Exercise. — Write a personal letter to the instructor, concerning some matter in which you would like to interest him. This letter will not be read to the class.

Written Exercise. — Write to some friend a long letter, observing the ordinary rules for paragraphing. Suggested subjects: an account of your life since last meeting your friend; a comparison of the town you now live in with that in which you and the friend formerly lived; an explanation of some scheme in which you wish the friend's co-operation.

CHAPTER XIII

REPRODUCTION, ABSTRACT, SUMMARY, ABRIDGMENT

Literal Reproduction. — The word *reproduction* is often used in Rhetoric in a somewhat general sense, to mean any version of another composition. As we shall use it, the term means *literal reproduction;* in other words, a version that follows the phrasing of the original as nearly as the time given for study will permit. Writing of reproductions trains the memory and adds immensely to one's command of words.

Below are given lists of brief selections most of them requiring not more than ten minutes to reproduce. It is suggested that a given paragraph or page be slowly read aloud to the class, two or three times, and that the class afterward write the piece as nearly as possible in the author's words. *Each student should then insert in his vocabulary book any new words or phrases that seem to him particularly serviceable. These memoranda will prove invaluable later on, when similar topics (not the same ones) are to be written about by the student himself.* To illus-

262

trate: a student after reading two or three personal descriptions might jot down for future use such phrases as the following: *Eyes.* — Laughing, startled, heavy-lidded, hazel, vacant, protruding, lustrous, expressive, liquid, dreamy, speaking, glad. *Nose.* — Aquiline, Roman, beak-like, shapely, snub, sharp, insignificant. *Hair.* — Grizzled, frowsy, shaggy, glossy, dishevelled, unkempt, tumbled. *Manner.* — Alert, jaunty, affable, sprightly, haughty, pretentious, modest, diffident, reserved, ostentatious, demure, animated. *Figure.* — Gaunt, emaciated, lank, vigorous, robust, grotesque, massive, insignificant, thiek-set, portly, sturdy, stalwart, erect, decrepit, fragile. *Expression.* — Rueful, crafty, frank, wistful, stolid.

MATERIAL FOR LITERAL REPRODUCTION

Narration

Miles, One Thousand and One Anecdotes: p. 30, Garcia; 33, Handel; 36, Mozart; 43, Paganini; 74, A dull witness; 96, Mrs. Siddons; 105, 110, Wellingtou; 106, Coolness; 132, Bad handwriting; 142, Dickens and Thackeray; 218, Hill; 231, Newton· 231, Sidney Smith; 251, Scott; 253, Lessing; 254, Geological; 255, Blackie; 268, Béranger; 273, A toast; 304, A careful reader; 312, Webster; 316, Johnson; 318, Poetry and Pattypans; 322, Marryat; 323, Turner; 324, Dannecker; 328, Hugo and

Coppée; 368, Heroism of a workman; 370, Roche-jaquelin; 371, Washington; 374, Lefevre; 378, Virchow; 378, Cham and Gille.

Description

Persons. — Hawthorne: American Note Books. See Index, p. 448, for paragraphs on characters, mostly men.

Scenery. — 1. *Sunrise.* Hawthorne: American Note Books, 75, 121, 315. Thoreau: Spring, 99.

2. *Morning.* Hawthorne: American Note Books, 75, 177. Thoreau: Winter, 128, 137, 258.

3. *Afternoon.* Hawthorne: American Note Books, 96. Thoreau: Autumn, 21, 28, 182.

4. *Sunset.* Hawthorne: American Note Books 112. Thoreau: Autumn, 3, 17, 90, 112, 152, 214, 259, 311, 327, 330, 345, 388, 429, 433. Winter, 23, 38, 40, 127, 155. Summer, 47, 246, 313, 332, 362.

5. *Sunlight.* Burroughs: Winter Sunshine, 102. Thoreau: Autumn, 289. Winter, 114, 249.

6. *Moonlight.* Hawthorne: The Scarlet Letter (Custom House). Ruskin: Præterita, vol. ii., 166. Thoreau: Spring, 78. Summer, 95, 97, 117, 120, 176, 233, 239, 333. Winter, 215, 320, 322. Burroughs: Winter Sunshine, 43.

7. *Water.* Blackmore: Lorna Doone, vii. Thoreau: Spring, 87, 96, 101, 109, 154. Summer, 30, 117, 240 , 243. Autumn, 111, 160, 182, 370, 400, 434. Ruskin: Præterita, vol. ii., 159 (The Rhone).

8. *Mountains.* Ruskin: Præterita, vol. i., 288. Bolles: At the North of Bearcamp Water. See Index, p. 296, for many views of more than a score of mountains.

9. *Landscapes.* Ruskin: Præterita, vol. ii., 78 (Rome). Hawthorne: American Note Books, 441 (Gosport). Blackmore: Lorna Doone, iv. (Doone Gate). Hugo: Les Misérables (Field of Waterloo).

Birds, Animals, and Insects. — See indexes of the following: Thoreau: Spring; Summer; Autumn; Winter; Walden. Burroughs: Wake Robin; Winter Sunshine; Birds and Bees. Miller: Bird-Ways; A Bird-Lover in the West. Torrey: A Rambler's Lease; Birds in the Bush. Merriam: A-Birding on a Broncho. Bolles: From Blomidon to Smoky; The Land of the Lingering Snow; At the North of Bearcamp Water. Gibson: Sharp Eyes.

Buildings and Rooms. — Ruskin: Præterita, vol. i., 232 (chapel); vol. iii., 5 (monastery). Scott: Ivanhoe, iii. (Saxon hall). Stevenson: An Inland Voyage (Noyon Cathedral); The Amateur Emigrant (the second cabin). Hawthorne: House of the Seven Gables, i.; Howe's Masquerade (the Province House). Irving: The Alhambra. (Palace of the Alhambra); Sketch Book (Westminster Abbey). Lamb: The East India Office.

Exposition

Helps: Thoughts in the Cloister and the Crowd, 14, 27, 32, 33, 40, 42, 54, 61, 72.   Brevia, 5, 14, 15, 22, 37, 91, 92, 94, 105, 113, 115, 161, 163.

Blake: Thoreau's Thoughts, 4, 9, 21, 46, 89, 98, 100, 103, 108, 118, 123.

Summary, Abstract, Abridgment. — The ability to arrive at the substance of an article or book and write it down, is demanded constantly in almost every business and in every profession.   An extremely brief statement of the substance is called a *summary*.   A longer statement, couched in language independent of that used by the author, is an *abstract*.   If the article or book is shortened by the omission of the less important parts, the language of the original being in general retained, the result is an *abridgment*.

Almost any well-constructed composition lends itself to summary, abstract, or abridgment.   A story of Irving or Hawthorne, a chapter of Parkman or John Fiske, an article in the *Forum* or the *Nation*, furnishes excellent material.   Below are given typical pieces that may be used, the shorter ones for summary, the longer for abstract or abridgment.   Stories can better be abstracted than abridged.

It is well to plan the proportions of your version.   The scale of **1 : 6** (one paragraph to six) will be found a good proportion on which to reduce the longer pieces. Burke's Speech On Conciliation would thus reduce to an abstract or an abridgment of about twenty paragraphs. But this speech can be reduced on a scale of **1 : 10** or even **1 : 20**.

MATERIAL FOR SUMMARY, ABSTRACT, ABRIDGMENT

Narration

1. *Personal Contests : — Spartacus and Hermann* A. J. Church: Two Thousand Years Ago, p. 31 ff. *Christian and Apollyon*, Bunyan: Pilgrim's Progress, Fourth Stage. *Archery*, Scott: Ivanhoe, xiii. *David and Goliath*, I Samuel xvii. *Nickleby and Squeers*, Dickens: Nicholas Nickleby, xiii. *The Boat Race*, Hughes: Tom Brown at Oxford. *Siege of the Round House*, Stevenson: Kidnapped, x. *The Three-Handed Duel*, Marryat: Midshipman Easy. *The Tournament*, Scott: Ivanhoe, xii.

2. *Narrative chapters from :* Aldrich: Story of a Bad Boy. Burnett: The One I Knew the Best of All. Hale: A New England Boyhood. Larcom: A New England Girlhood. Howells: My Year in a Log Cabin. Warner: Being a Boy.

3. *Stories.* — Hawthorne: The Snow Image; The Great Stone Face; Ethan Brand; Legends of the Province House; The Great Carbuncle; David Swan; The Vision of the Fountain; Dr. Heidegger's Experiment; The Artist of the Beautiful.

Wilkins: A Humble Romance; The Bar Lighthouse; A Lover of Flowers; Gentian; A Conflict Ended; A Village Singer; Sister Liddy; A Gala Dress; A Village Lear; The Revolt of Mother.

Sir Roger de Coverley Papers: Spectators No. 110, 112, 113, 116, 118, 122, 123, 132, 269, 329, 335, 359, 383, 517.

4. *History.* — Green: History of the English People. *Bæda*, vol. i., ch. 2, pp. 64–67. *Hastings*, vol. i., ch. 4, pp. 113–114. *Rising of baronage*, B. iii., ch. 1, pp. 240–244. *Calais*, B. iv., ch. 2, pp. 422–425. *Armada*, B. vi., ch. 6, pp. 444–446. *Return of Napoleon; Waterloo*, B. ix., ch. 5, pp. 385–389.

McMasters: History of the People of the United States. *Marietta*, vol. i., 513–515. *Death of Hamilton*, vol. iii., 52–53. *Leopard and Chesapeake*, vol. iii., 258–259. *Monroe's journey*, vol. iv., 377–380.

Fiske: Critical Period of American History. The Continental Congress, vol. i., ch. 3. Valley Forge, vol. ii., ch. 9.

Rolfe, W. J.: Tales from English History in Prose and Verse.

Yonge: Book of Golden Deeds.

Description

1. *Schools.* — See The Schoolmaster in Literature. (American Book Co.)

2. *Towns.* — Hale: Seven Spanish Cities. Howells: Three Villages; A Boy's Town. Stedman:

New York City (*St. Nicholas*, 20 : 403, '93). Stockton : St. Augustine (*Ibid.*, 21 : 206, '94).

Exposition. — 1. Nordhoff: Politics for Young Americans. 2. Van Dyke: How to judge a picture. 3. Krehbiel: How to understand music. 4. Wagner: Courage. 5. Camp: American Football. 6. Stagg and Williams: American Football. 7. Bassett: Machinist's trade (*Harper's Young People*, 64 : 682, '91). The Printing Trade (*Ibid.*, 64 : 624, '91). The following articles from *The Youth's Companion:* 8. Journalism for girls (64 : 657, '91). 9. Civil Service (64 : 245, '91). 10. Why men must die (67 : 426, '94). 11. Medicine as a profession (64 : 258, '91). 12. Success in railway life (65 : 505, '92). 13. Wholesome lunches (67 : 83, '94). 14–18. Advice to young musicians (64 : 310, 418, 321, 362). 19. Separate functions of the Senate and House of Representatives (63 : 633, '90). 20. Self-Education (65 : 494, '92). 21–23. The girl who thinks she can write (64 : 447 ; 65 : 458, 734). 24. Trusts (67 : 538, '94). 25. Uses of the census (63 : 89, '90). 26. Monroe Doctrine (67 : 388, '94). 27. Arbitration (67 : 48, '94). 28. Good government clubs (67 : 448, '94).

Argument[1]

1. A property qualification for municipal suffrage is desirable.

[1] The first four subjects are taken from Brookings and Ringwalt : *Briefs for Debate* (Longmans), which see for further

Affirmative. White: *Forum*, x. 357 (Dec. 1890).
Eliot: *Forum*, xii. 153 (Oct. 1891).
Negative. Bryce: American Commonwealth, i.,
chaps. i., iii.

2. An eight-hour working day should be adopted
by law.

Affirmative. Webb and Cox: The Eight Hours
Day.
Negative. Walker: Atlantic Monthly, lxv. 800
(June, 1890).

3. Municipalities should sometimes give work
to the unemployed.

Affirmative. *Forum*, xvi. 655 (Feb. 1894). Coit
Forum, xvii. 276 (May, 1894).
Negative. *Nation*, lvii. 481 (Dec. 28, 1893).

4. The housing of the poor should be improved
by municipalities.

Affirmative. Riis: How the Other Half Lives.
Negative. White: Improved Dwellings for the
Laboring Classes.

5. Burke: On Conciliation with the American
Colonies.

6. Chatham: On Removing Troops from Boston.[1]

7. Beecher: Liverpool Speech.[1]

[1] See Baker: *Specimens of Modern Argumentation* (Henry
Holt & Co.).

CHAPTER XIV

NARRATION AND DESCRIPTION

Narration, or narrative, relates a series of events. Description gives an account of the look of persons or things. Character description gives both physical and mental traits. Recall to memory various stories you have read, and say whether narratives of considerable length do or do not have to give description as they proceed.

NARRATION

Two Kinds. — If a series of events actually happened, they are historical, and the story of them may be called *historical narrative*. If they did not happen, but owe their existence to the imagination, they are fictional, and the narrative is *fiction*. If we are writing a story, let the fact be understood; if a sober rehearsal of facts, let it be made an exercise in the rare and difficult art of truth-telling.

Exercises in Choice of Subject. — (1) Examine a daily paper and pick out several narratives which seem to you to have a general human interest,

271

and several that have not. (2) Write a list of twenty subjects for narrative and submit them to the class for a vote as to which are the most interesting. Choose events which you have witnessed or taken part in. (3) Write a list of what are to you the most interesting events of ancient, mediæval, and modern history.

Choice of Details. — In writing an account of a simple incident it is possible to tell every detail of what happened. But evidently no such thing is practicable in narrating the events of a day, a week, a lifetime. What to omit will depend much upon the length of the composition. A clear-headed writer will not put pen to paper before he has decided just what points he is going to bring out.

Written Exercise. — (1) Jot down on paper memoranda of the important things, the turning events, in your own past life. (2) Make memoranda to show what events ought to stand out most distinctly in a history of the United States.

Plot. — Read the following : —

Ichabod Crane was ridiculously frightened one dark night by a boy who played ghost. The lad took the part of a traditional spectre that rode a black horse. The joker had a cloak over his head, and before him on the saddle a pumpkin, to represent the head which the headless horseman was fabled to carry.

Read now the following : —

One dark night Ichabod Crane started homeward on horse-back.   He approached the oak on which André, the spy, was hanged.   Ichabod's heart quaked.   He passed the haunted tree in safety, but his heart almost stood still when, a little farther on, he saw a strange rider on a gigantic horse.   Horse and rider kept pace with him.   Ichabod however saw that the latter was headless, nay, carried his head before him on the saddle.   The figure raised itself and hurled its head at Ichabod.   When the schoolmaster found himself on the ground, did he realize that the grewsome missile was only a pumpkin ?

Which of these accounts begets *suspense as to the outcome ?*   In other words, in which is there *plot ?*   Recall some novel you have read, and explain how the reader's interest is held through to the end.

Oral Exercise. — Recall some anecdote, and present it orally with plot interest.

Theme. — Write a simple historical narrative of about two hundred words, giving without plot all the details of some brief incident in your own experience.   The following may suggest a topic : 1. My first day at the lathe.   2. Examination memories.   3. How I earned some money and how I spent it.   4. Spearing fish by night.   5. A personal adventure with a window.   6. How I spent this morning.

Theme. — Write one or more imaginary news-paper items, without plot, each detailing some

simple incident.   Choose a subject of local interest
if possible.   For example: 1. A runaway. 2. Fire
on Seventh Street. 3. Trolley-car accident. 4. Curious act of a bird.   5. April 23 at the Brown School.
6. Brave deed of a child.   7. He returned $500.
8. An old building demolished.   9. The new library
is opened.   10. Arrested for " scorching."

Themes. — Select several topics for five hundred
word themes, and write outlines showing what details you would emphasize in composing.   Then
write historical narratives from the outlines, making
them as interesting as you can without deviating
from facts.   Sample subjects: 1. My struggles
with cooking. 2. A day in the berry patch. 3. The
first time I saw a play.   4. An adventure of my
father. 5. A few days with a doctor.   6. How a
certain town was named.   7. Misfortunes of our
circus. 8. The tribulations of a truant. 9. My first
ocean voyage. 10. An uncomfortable call.   11. My
career as an actor.   12. A visit to the World's Fair.
13. In a graveyard after dark.   14. How Smith
looked me up. 15. A week in the woods.   16. The
fall I had.   17. My experience as a clerk.   18. A
glimpse of college life.   19. What I saw some bees
do. 20. An unwilling swim. 21. That Fourth of
July. 22. Experiences with a pony. 23. Haying.
24. How the vacation passed.   25. When I was a
book-agent.   26. Crossing a swollen stream.

Complex Incident. — Many a narrative must be composed of several *threads*, telling different events that were going on at the same time. If you were giving an account of how two hunters after being separated in the woods finally reached home again, you would relate first how one got home, then how the other got home; or, having narrated the wanderings of the first, you would let the second tell his own story on rejoining his companion.

Theme. — Relate a complex incident, either historical or fictional, in a theme about five hundred words long. Two or three threads are enough. The following may suggest a subject: 1. Two roads to town. 2. How our party reached the top of the mountain. 3. Adventures of a lost child and its parents. 4. The rescue of an amateur sailor from a wreck. 5. What happened at our club meeting. 6. Three boys and a boat. 7. An overheard discussion.

DESCRIPTION

Language is better adapted to narrate than to describe, for words follow each other, just as events do; they cannot flash the whole picture, with all the details, upon the reader. Consequently writers often combine narrative and description in order to dwell on details. Homer[1] describes the shield of Achilles by telling the story of its forging — how

---

[1] *Iliad*, xviii. 601, Bryant's translation.

Vulcan wrought each part in turn. What is called the *traveller's view* is description from successive points of view. There is a good example of this kind of description in Hawthorne's *American Note Books*, p. 181.

In some descriptions the writer is willing to sacrifice the general look of the object, in order to secure accuracy of detail. Giving each detail is called *description by inventory*. This is often useful, particularly in business or in science. Turn to any book of natural history and read the inventory description of some bird or animal. But ordinarily a description should give a general impression whether it afterward gives details or not. The most common way of doing this is to tell what in general the object to be described makes you think of. If the object is a river, it may remind you of a snake or a letter S; if a village, it may recall to your mind a flat-iron; if a little old lady, it may appear to you, as to Dickens, in *Hard Times*, "a bundle of shawls." The main impression thus received is called the *fundamental image.*

Not every object will furnish a fundamental image, but every object is sure to be remembered for a few *chief details.* If of a given landscape there lingers in the memory only a dim sense of green woods, with here and there a patch of white, it is as much description to record this dim image as it would be to detail kinds of trees, distances, etc. Indeed, it is a mistake often made to report in a description things that could not possibly have been seen from the given point of view. To *keep the point of view* is vital. It is a good practice to describe a photograph — such as those published by the Soule Company, of Boston — in order to learn the art of proportion in these matters of living details.

It must not however, be thought that details have no place in description. In studying an object with a view to writing about it, one should have the eye of a hawk for every *visible* detail, in order that what he writes may be truthful. There is no better training for the powers of observation than description. Send a careless person to the lake to describe it. He reports " myriads of ripples dancing in glee," things that every wretched poetaster has seen before him. Send a careful observer, and he will report wonderful shades of color, and curious surface effects, like corrugation and damascene.

Suggested Topics for Description

By Inventory. — 1. The bluebird. 2. A jellyfish. 3. A luna moth. 4. Kinds of clouds. 5. In a museum. 6. Flags of different nations. 7. A bottle of ink. 8. A small boy's pocket. 9. What my room contains. 10. A shop window. 11. The old swimming-hole. 12. A bit of old silver.

By Narrative. — 1. A day in Boston. 2. An oil well. 3. A crowd. 4. A quaint tea party. 5. A country fair. 6. A fire. 7. A dream. 8. The matinée. 9. A masquerade. 10. How the farm looked when I went back. 11. The dynamo I made. 12. My tent-making. 13. Our hut. 14. Decorating a church for Christmas. 15. My baking. 16. Up Pike's Peak.

By Fundamental Image and Details. — 1. Kinds of noses. 2. A bit of old architecture. 3. A church altar. 4. Famous deltas. 5. The shop. 6. The lunch-room. 7. A little old man. 8. This town in A.D. 2000. 9. An old fireplace. 10. A wreck. 11. Profile Mountain. 12. The football field. 13. The baseball ground described for an Englishman. 14. The capitol. 15. An old horse.

By Chief Details. — 1. Uncle Billy. 2. A hermit. 3. Our postmaster. 4. Our mail-carrier. 5. An Indian. 6. A southern girl. 7. My chum. 8. The procession of the pines. 9. A moonlight scene. 10. A wood interior. 11. An American boy of 1925. 12. Houses I have lived in. 13. Two generals. 14. The boy who grins. 15. Queer street characters. 16. A cat. 17. The fortune-teller. 18. Curious advertisements. 19. Betty in her best dress. 20. A sunset. 21. A wave.

CHAPTER XV

EXPOSITION AND ARGUMENT

EXPOSITION

Exposition is explanation. It may either explain a general principle by illustrations and examples, as the preacher's sermon expounds a statement of scripture, or it may explain a group of facts by getting at their underlying principle, as a scientific treatise does. Exposition, it is clear, deals with ideas rather than with particular objects. We describe a department store; we expound the principles by which it is conducted. We describe an electric motor; we expound the laws of electricity. We describe a beautiful statue; we expound beauty.

Below are given various subjects for exposition. In writing about them, do not drift into argument. If you write on "dangers of exercise," do not argue against over-exercise; calmly explain the matter.

Subjects for Exposition

1. Golf. 2. Cannibalism. 3. The bear family. 4. Principles of diet. 5. Credulity. 6. Nostalgia. 7. How to sail a boat. 8. Drowned rivers. 9. On

eating candy. 10. The formation of ravines.
11. Dangers of over-exercise. 12. Dangers of
too little exercise. 13. Why the earth quakes.
14. How men become criminals. 15. How the
will may be trained in the classroom. 16. An
ideal classroom. 17. What makes up an ideal
camping ground. 18. Advantages and disadvan-
tages of classroom study. 19. Effects of climate
on man. 20. The conduct of a great business.
21. What are home missions? 22. How to become famous. 23. How to plan a dinner. 24. How
to furnish a sitting-room. 25. Advantages of small
classes. 26. Possibilities of electricity. 27. What
constitutes a great man? 28. The art of fly-casting.
29. The construction of a roof. 30. What good
does an examination do the student? 31. Spiritu-
alism. 32. Ghosts. 33. My choice of a profession.
34. The banking system. 35. Practical values of
good manners. 36. The interpretation of any of
the proverbs given on pages 213–215.

ARGUMENT

There are various ways of bringing people to our
way of thinking. One way, by appealing to their
reason, is called *argument*. Can you suggest other
ways?

Every argument must have a *proposition*, which
is laid down to be proved. If this proposition is
not stated in the title of the argument, it should be

stated early in the discussion. It cannot be too definitely formulated. Every word of it should be made clear; there should be full *exposition of terms.* Half the quarrels in the world disappear after a thorough definition of terms. The question of whether Aaron Burr was guilty of treason depends on how treason is defined. In law a man, however traitorous, is not guilty of treason unless his treason had been witnessed by two persons. Burr's treason was not witnessed; he escaped conviction.[1]

In argument (*a*) depend upon a few weighty arguments rather than upon many weak ones; (*b*) remember that *examples* are but weak arguments; (*c*) if in debate, be perfectly fair to your opponent, admitting all that is true on his side; (*d*) know your case thoroughly in every detail.

Subjects for Argument or Debate

1. Examinations are usually a fair test of scholarship. **2.** Labor-saving machinery is a permanent advantage to mankind. **3.** The world owes every man a living. **4.** A truthful person will be a better writer than a liar. **5.** The Gulf of Mexico will one day have a greater port than New York now has. **6.** High school students should read the newspapers. **7.** Observation helps us more than

[1] Carpenter and Fletcher, *Introduction to Theme-Writing,* p. 117.

reading.   8. Examinations should be abolished.
9. Sunday observance should be compulsory.   10. A
high school is guilty of injustice to its students
if it does not train them in public speaking.
11. People possessing no property should not be
allowed to vote.   12. Is it right to break a friendship ?   13. Ought department stores to be permitted ?   14. Are there good excuses for being a
tramp ?   15. Is it wrong to bet ?   16. How far is
it right in politics that to the victors should belong
the spoils ?   17. Should a parent forbid his son to
take part in football ?   18. Should a man ever shoot
a robber ?   19. Is suicide ever justifiable ?   20. Is it
right to evade custom house duties ?   21. Is it
wrong to go to the theatre often ?   22. Is it ever
best to give money on the street ?   23. Is it right
for women to wear birds on their hats ?   24. How
far is it right for students to study together ?
25. Is a curfew law desirable ?   26. Is it right to
discard old friends for new ?   27. Should one bear
witness against a friend ?   28. Does paying a fare
entitle one to a seat ?   29. Is it right to let people
deceive themselves ?   30. Are there any customary
lies which are right ?   31. Is capital punishment
defensible as punishment ?   32. Is capital punishment defensible as a protection to society ?
33. Should Latin be a compulsory study ?
34. Which is rougher, football or pugilism ?

SUBJECT INDEX

INDEX OF AUTHORS QUOTED

EXERCISES IN RHETORIC

AND

ENGLISH COMPOSITION.

BY

GEORGE R. CARPENTER,

Professor of Rhetoric and English Composition, Columbia College.

HIGH-SCHOOL COURSE.   SEVENTH EDITION.

16mo. Cloth. Price 75 cents, net.

ADVANCED COURSE.   FOURTH EDITION.

12mo. Cloth. Price $1.00, net.

" This work gives the student the very gist and germ of the art of composition." — *Public Opinion.*

" G. R. Carpenter, Professor of Rhetoric and English Composition in Columbia College, has prepared a work under the title of ' Exercises in Rhetoric and English Composition,' in which not so much the science of Rhetoric is mapped out and defined as the practical workings of the art are furnished to the student with just enough of the principles to guide him aright The author gives an abundance of exercises for the student to study and analyze, and this is the very best kind of help. The scheme of the subject-matter is somewhat unique and novel, but it is comprehensive and lucid. . . . A very serviceable and suggestive book to read and consult " — *Education.*

" The text represents the substance of teaching which a freshman may fairly be expected to compass, and it is set forth with a clearness and directness and brevity so admirable as to make the volume seem almost the realization of that impossible short method of learning to write which has often been sought for, but never with a nearer approach to being found. . . . We do not hesitate to give unreserved commendation to this little book." — *The Nation.*

" Seldom has so much good common sense been put within so brief a space." — *The Boston Herald.*

THE MACMILLAN COMPANY,

66 FIFTH AVENUE, NEW YORK.

THE ENGLISH POETS.

WITH CRITICAL INTRODUCTIONS BY VARIOUS WRITERS AND A GENERAL INTRODUCTION BY

MATTHEW ARNOLD.

EDITED BY

THOMAS HUMPHRY WARD, M.A.

In Four Volumes. 12mo.

Vol. I. Chaucer to Donne. Vol. III. Addison to Blake.
Vol. II. Ben Jonson to Dryden. Vol. IV. Wordsworth to Tennyson.

Cabinet Edition. Four Volumes in Box, $5.00.
Student's Edition. Each Volume sold separately. $1.00 per vol.

" All lovers of poetry, all students of literature, all readers, will welcome the volumes of 'The English Poets.' . . . Mr. Matthew Arnold has written a most delightful introduction, full of wise thought and poetic sensibility. Very few books can be named in which so much that is precious can be had in so little space and for so little money." — *Philadelphia Times.*

"Altogether it would be difficult to select four volumes of any kind better worth owning and studying than these." *Nation.*

"These four volumes ought to be placed in every library, and, if possible, in the hands of every student of English." — *Churchman.*

" Ward's ' English Poets ' has been acknowledged to be one of the most serviceable and discriminating contributions to the history of English poetry." — *Quips.*

THE MACMILLAN COMPANY,

66 FIFTH AVENUE, NEW YORK.

ENGLISH PROSE

SELECTIONS WITH CRITICAL INTRODUCTIONS BY VARIOUS WRITERS,
AND GENERAL INTRODUCTIONS TO EACH PERIOD.

EDITED BY

HENRY CRAIK, LL.D.

In Five Volumes. 12mo.

Volume   I. From the Fourteenth to the Sixteenth Century.
Volume II. The Sixteenth Century to the Restoration.
Volume III. The Seventeenth Century.
Volume IV. The Eighteenth Century.
Volume V. Nineteenth Century from Sir Walter Scott to
    Robert Louis Stevenson.

Cabinet Edition. Five Volumes in Box, $7.50.

Student's Edition. Each Volume sold separately. $1.10 per vol.

COMMENTS.

" If prose literature can ever be successfully studied by means of short extracts, it will be possible to conduct such a study with the aid of this book. As a companion book of Ward's 'English Poets' it is very interesting and satisfactory. In the Department of Rhetoric, this book will certainly be of greater value than any other work of the kind yet published."— PROF. H. H. NEILL, *Amherst College.*

" Mr. Craik and his coadjutors do their work admirably. Their remarks are appropriate, their selection of extracts is felicitous. We thank them for not a few happy hours."— *Literary World.*

" The extracts are carefully chosen and edited, and a brief sketch of each writer is given. These sketches are written by men who edit the different sections, and as these men are selected from the foremost of English critics, the result is that the books contain a valuable set of brief essays from able and distinguished pens. George Saintsbury, Alfred Ainger, Edmund Gosse, Norman Moore, and others besides the editor himself have contributed, and the book would have been valuable did it contain nothing but these introductory notices. The conclusions of the editors of the different authors who have summed up the characteristics of the separate men represented in the previous volume, have done their work so well, that the student is likely in the end to have a rather better idea of the writers than he would gather from his unaided study of the original and complete works of these old writers."— *Boston Courier.*

THE MACMILLAN COMPANY,

66 FIFTH AVENUE, NEW YORK.

THE HISTORY

OF THE

ENGLISH LANGUAGE

BY

OLIVER FARRAR EMERSON, A.M., Ph.D.,

Assistant Professor of Rhetoric and English Philology in Cornell University.

Second Edition, Revised. 12mo. pp. 415. Cloth. Price $1.25, net.

"A work that, as a treatise for the instruction of the individual student as well as for class-room use, is to be warmly commended. . . . On every page of this admirably arranged volume is shown the fruit of original thought, profound erudition, and philosophical grasp of a subject which has been too often obscured by injudicious counsel." — *The Beacon.*

"An admirable work; the best results of recent research are embodied in it." *Providence Journal.*

"The work is a valuable contribution to linguistic science, and it will be a welcome text-book in colleges and schools and to all students of philology" *Home Journal.*

"In respect both of scholarship and of exposition, this volume is entitled to high praise. . . . There is no part of this book that cannot be read with pleasure as well as profit, and one is therefore embarrassed by the wealth of material worthy of illustration" — *New York Sun.*

THE MACMILLAN COMPANY,

66 FIFTH AVENUE, NEW YORK.

Made in the USA
Las Vegas, NV
13 September 2021